THE LIVES OF AUTHORS

By the Same Author

*

MORE COMPANIONABLE BOOKS

General.

This Boo...

THE
LIVES OF AUTHORS

GEORGE GORDON

1950

Chatto and Windus

LONDON

PUBLISHED BY

Chatto & Windus

LONDON

*

Clarke, Irwin & Co. Ltd.

TORONTO

Preface

A FAMILIAR object on my husband's shelves was a large portfolio, inscribed L/A. It contained, along with his comments and reflections, passages concerning the art of biography and the lives of authors which had caught his attention in the course of his reading over many years. It was the nursery of many of the essays in this book which, therefore, has borrowed its title, *The Lives of Authors*. His pen served readily those authors—the Elizabethan Ralegh, St. Evremond and others—who shared his zest for living. His conviction that literature consists of men and things led naturally to this lifelong interest in biography, and gives unity to these various studies, ranging from early papers to the work of his mature years.

Some of these essays are unrevised by their author. His standard of accuracy and finish was known to be high. 'When fact and fine writing quarrel,' he would say, 'it is up with fact and down with finery.' If, therefore, inaccuracies are to be found, the blame must lie at my door. My task, however, has been eased by the kindness of Mr. C. H. Wilkinson, Dr. L. F. Powell, Professor Nichol Smith, and Professor E. N. da C. Andrade, who have helped me in tracing and verifying quoted passages. I am indebted also to Mr. H. W. Garrod for his translation of Milton's Latin verses on p. 55, and to Mr. E. C. Gregory for his advice in the selection of the essays.

I wish to thank the Curators of the Taylor Institution for allowing me to print the Taylorian Lecture on St. Evremond, and to acknowledge also the courtesy of the several publishers who have granted permission to reprint various essays in this volume.

MARY GORDON

Contents

THE LIVES OF AUTHORS

THE LIVES OF AUTHORS

I HAVE often asked myself what it is that makes people so curious about authors. Many readers, of course, are not; they take their dose of print as they take their tobacco or their meals, and regard the name of the author as only one of many trademarks. They order in almost precisely the same spirit another box of cigarettes and another P. G. Wodehouse. To this enormous class of readers the life of a professional author, when they think of it at all (which is seldom), seems as odd and remote as the life of a financier or a company promoter does to me. I accept the fact and the mystery of money as they accept the fact and the mystery of books, and we both leave it at that.

I have, let me say, no quarrel with this class of readers. Indeed, I like them. They are the clay we grow our roses in. They are the imperturbable force of gravity which keeps our mimic world, the coterie world of the Arts, from flying off into fragments. They keep authors in their place at the same time as they contribute to their support. Being purely customers, they steadily remind us of what authors and their votaries have often tended, I think unhealthily, to conceal: the plain fact that, whatever else it is, professional authorship at any rate is in one important aspect of it a business, in which something, however valuable, is offered for sale. The price may be ludicrous—a few coins for an immortal composition; but still we are asked to buy. We put down our money for it; it does not come to us in a vision, or with the dew. Even a poet sells his works, if he can, and has been known to compare his takings with those of other poets. Lord Tennyson had made great sacrifices for his art; he was a *vates sacer*, a dedicated bard. But he knew exactly what Longfellow's publishers gave him as a retaining fee, and it annoyed him extremely, and justifiably, that his own was less.

There remains, of our gigantic reading public, a still considerable portion which looks behind the commodity, and cannot help being interested in the authors of the books it reads. It is a natural curiosity, though some decry it as impertinent. 'You have the book,' they say; 'why muddle the impression by calling in the author?' But most books that are worth anything are a barter of experience, and it is not unreasonable, I think, that one should wish to test sincerity, to check credentials. I believe that women, on the whole, have been quicker to ask for this than men, which is what we should expect. They have very good and particular reasons for being interested in sincerity. Women less often than men forget the speaker in the speech, and they have always been more attracted by persons than by principles. In the matter of authors, and more especially of the lives of authors, this bias of women has been important. 'I have observed,' says Addison, in that well-known first sentence of the *Spectator*, 'that a reader seldom peruses a book with pleasure until he knows whether the writer of it be a black or a fair man, of a mild or choleric disposition, married or a bachelor, with other particulars of the like nature that conduce very much to the right understanding of an author.' This, no doubt, was mainly Addison's fun, but it was also a recognition of something genuine and novel. The empire of the leisured reading public had begun its slow passage into the hands of women, where, in England and America at any rate, it now rests. As women became readers, let us say, the lives of authors became interesting. For it is not, I would have you observe, a male curiosity that Addison describes. The particulars cited are not men's particulars. 'Black' or 'fair,' 'married' or 'a bachelor,' no male reader cares twopence about this. The curiosity is feminine. I believe that the persistent pressure of this natural inquisitiveness has had almost as much to do with the development of literary biography as the scholarly and historical interests of men.

What Addison could not foresee was that this child of curiosity should so marvellously outgrow its parents, that the lives of authors should become, as in the last hundred

2

years they have become, an exciting topic in themselves, quite apart from the works which presumably they illustrate. Boswell's *Life of Johnson* is read from many motives, and any motive will do, but rarely, even now, because it conduces to an understanding of *The Rambler*. The lives of Burns and Cowper, of Byron and Shelley, of Keats and Wordsworth, are not only by many people better known than their works; they are actually better known than the lives of even the greatest of their contemporaries who did not also happen to be famous authors. And I ask myself why.

Whatever the reason, the thing itself is revolutionary. Until the eighteenth century or the closing years of the seventeenth, an author, certainly an English author, to have his life written, had to be notable, as a rule, in some other way. He must be a statesman, or a soldier, or a divine, and under cover of this distinction his literary life might be portrayed. I wish that this plain historical fact were better known. We should have been saved so much nonsense about the 'mystery' of the life of Shakespeare, the great Stratford riddle. Beyond the miracle of transcendent genius there is no 'mystery' about Shakespeare's life. Biographically his state is normal. We know less about his elder contemporary Spenser, who moved in official circles, and for many years had been by general consent the greatest poet of his age. Literary biography, as we understand it, was not yet a felt need. Even a century later it seemed to be no one's business to write a life of John Dryden, the ruling writer of his day, and we know in consequence very little about him beyond what he has told us himself. What Johnson says of Dryden may be said, indeed, of nearly all our English writers before the eighteenth century: 'His contemporaries, however they reverenced his genius, left his life unwritten; and nothing therefore can be known beyond what casual mention and uncertain tradition have supplied.'

We have reversed all that, and reversed it so violently that it is now not the authors who are in shadow, but those very public men who formerly obscured them. For one person to-day who knows anything, for example, of the lives of the great statesmen and other public characters of the last two centuries, of the Walpoles and Chathams, the Castlereaghs and Palmerstons, there are fifty who know the lives, or something about the lives, of the distinguished contemporary writers whom these potentates ignored or patronized. And the reason? Are authors, as being by nature less reticent than other men, accomplices in the matter? To some extent, no doubt, they are, and to an increasing degree. Are they also, possibly, more interesting in themselves? I am inclined to suppose they must be, though, if this be so, it is a fairly modern discovery. The test of one's contemporaries gives rather doubtful results. Your experience may be different. But the professional authors of my acquaintance, the eminent living writers whom I am privileged to know, have never seemed to me, as a class, the most interesting men extant. Yet, when they die, the same thing, no doubt, will happen. Their often greater contemporaries in other walks of life will sink to a meagre entry in the biographical dictionaries, if indeed they are mentioned there at all, while researchers rake the dustbins for every rejected scrap from the writer's pen, and pursue him in biography from the premonitions of the nursery to the last lessons of the grave.

The holding acquired by authors in the biographical stock of the country is thus immense, for the effects of the new interest have been retrospective. The *Dictionary of National Biography* affords a rough and ready test of biographical standing. Apply it, and you will find that, in this particular competition, no class can hold a candle to the authors. As Walter Raleigh used to say, the gates that refuse to open for a minor canon open easily for the minor poet. Even the sailor, the soldier, the diplomatist must do magnificently more than his duty, or disastrously less, to gain admittance there. The rich merchant, who controlled in his time the prosperity of thousands, is turned away, while the poor author stretches himself at ease on the lap of posterity. Grub Street gives up its dead. We had a King in England once who, unless he is traduced, died of eating too many lampreys. We had also a poor author who died of eating too many red herrings. In the biographical dictionaries poor Green's red herrings now compete for immortality with the lampreys of King Henry.

I am not, of course, complaining. I do not fight with the tides. I only remark that biographical immortality seems to be purchased at different rates, and that the average rate for authors is not high. Their minimum rate is perhaps the lowest there is.

Can I explain it? Not entirely. To some extent, no doubt, there is trade unionism in the matter: authors write up authors. But in the end, I suppose, it is *expression* that does it. The smallest author who sincerely expresses his pin-point of a soul has, on this reckoning, more chance of survival than the dominant man who has never learned to confess, to commit himself to paper. So many great men are silent, or ill-equipped with words. Some of the most interesting lives of the last hundred years have been the lives of business men, but who is to write them? They cannot or will not do it themselves, and no author can do it for them. They survive as a rule only in the name and tradition of their firms, or in the titles of their benefactions. Hazlitt, it appears, was right. Authors are a longer-lived race than other men, because 'words are the only things that last for ever.'

Yet the authors, to do them justice, have never been happy about it. They know that action, 'fine doing,' is the finest thing in the world. 'We talked of war. *Johnson:* Every man thinks meanly of himself for not having been a soldier, or not having been at sea. *Boswell:* Lord Mansfield does not. *Johnson:* Sir, if Lord Mansfield were in a company of General Officers and Admirals who have been in service, he would shrink; he'd wish to creep under the table. *Boswell:* No; he'd think he could *try* them all. *Johnson:* . . . No, Sir; were Socrates and Charles the Twelfth of Sweden both present in any company, and Socrates to say, "Follow me, and hear a lecture on philosophy"; and Charles, laying his hand on his sword, to say, "Follow me, and dethrone the Czar"; a man would be ashamed to follow Socrates. Sir, the impression is universal; yet it is strange.' Just so, in Disraeli's *Lothair*, 'the

5

standing committee of the Holy Alliance of Peoples all rose, although they were extreme Republicans, when the General entered. Such' (says the author) 'is the magical influence of a man of action over men of the pen and the tongue.'

The votaries of literature tend to conceal these things and to assign a contemporary altitude to authors which now and then, indeed, may ideally have been theirs, but which in real life few of any generation have either possessed or claimed. There is a widespread habit among literary historians of naming what we call an 'Age' after its principal author— the Age of Johnson, the Age of Tennyson, and so on. It is a harmless enough habit when confined to its immediate purpose, and it is very convenient. But it is based, of course, on a historical unreality, and when thoughtlessly used, as it very often is, encourages the oddest misconceptions.

One reason, and not the least, for the slow development of literary biography was the doubtful standing of the professional author. To write for money was not genteel. Even so late as the middle of last century, Charlotte Yonge, for example, that popular Victorian authoress, could not touch her profits. A Yonge couldn't do that. Then the life, the mode of existence, of a professional author has few of those regular and tangible signs by which a community recognizes the props and pillars of its society. The very advantages of an author's trade work against him here. Let me recite them to you in the words of Trollope:

'There is perhaps no career of life,' he says, 'so charming as that of a successful man of letters. In the first place, you have such freedom: If you like the town, live in the town, and do your work there; if you like the country, choose the country. It may be done on the top of a mountain or in the bottom of a pit. It is compatible with the rolling of the sea and the motion of a railway. The clergyman, the lawyer, the doctor, the member of Parliament, the clerk in a public office, the tradesman, and even his assistant in the shop, must dress in accordance with certain fixed laws [the year was 1876]; but the author need sacrifice to no grace, hardly even to Propriety. He is subject to no bonds such as those which bind other men. Who else is free from all shackles as to hours? The judge must sit at ten, and the attorney-general, who is making his £20,000 a year, must be there with his bag. The Prime Minister must be in his place on that weary front bench shortly after prayers, and must sit there, either asleep or awake, even though —— or —— should be addressing the House. During all that Sunday which he maintains should be a day of rest, the active clergyman is toiling like a galley-slave. The actor, when eight o'clock comes, is bound to his footlights. The Civil Service clerk must sit there from ten till four—unless his office be fashionable, when twelve to six is just as heavy on him. The author may do his work at five in the morning when he is fresh from his bed, or at three in the morning before he goes there. . . ."

So Trollope runs on, and it is nearly all true. But of course, this very freedom, by removing the author from public check and control, only intensified the common doubt. Even to this day, among simple or old-fashioned people, the profession of author is apt to seem a dubious trade. When Thomas Hardy died, one of his cousins (I think it was), Miss Teresa Hardy, said to a reporter: 'Poor Tom! he was a clever boy, but I never thought he would have taken to writing. Writing, I think, is not a respectable way of earning a living.' Hardy, you see, had been bred an architect, and his family, it appears, would have preferred that he had remained one. So in Kirriemuir, some fifty years ago, there was consternation among the village elders when James Barrie set up as writer and as nothing else. 'Mercy be here!' said the old ladies, 'An author! And him an M.A.!' He might so preferably, with that appendage, have been a schoolmaster, a doctor, a clergyman—good visible occupations. In turning professional author he was thought to have stepped down.

This very natural feeling is no doubt fast disappearing. But it still lingers in unexpected quarters. When Mr. J. B. Priestley was writing *The Good Companions* in the village of Church Handborough, and spending long days thumping out that joyous work on his typewriter, the villagers, in the absence of any other explanation, felt obliged to conclude

7

the worst, and were divided in opinion whether he was a bookmaker or a begging letter-writer.

To return to the public interest in authors. One of the principal reasons for the change of fashion in that matter is the prevalent notion that the writer of an interesting book must be interesting in himself. Authors, of course, know better; it is so painfully possible that his book is the only interesting thing about him. Dr. Johnson was once asked by a certain Mrs. Cotterell to introduce her to a celebrated writer, and it is recorded that he dissuaded her from the attempt. 'Dearest madam,' he said, 'you had better let it alone; the best part of every author is in general to be found in his book.' So convinced was he of this that he recommends, indeed, to authors the great advantage of keeping out of sight: 'It has been long the custom of the oriental monarchs to hide themselves . . . and to be known to their subjects only by their edicts. The same policy is no less necessary to him that writes.' 'A transition,' he concludes, 'from an author's book to his conversation is too often like an entrance into a large city, after a distant prospect. Remotely, we see nothing but spires of temples, and turrets of palaces, and imagine it the residence of splendour, grandeur, and magnificence; but, when we have passed the gates, we find it perplexed with narrow passages, disgraced with despicable cottages, embarrassed with obstructions, and clouded with smoke.'

Since Johnson's time the exploration of those narrow passages in the lives of authors has become one of our literary industries. The results, on the whole, though highly interesting, have not tended to edification, and to a rather serious extent have been actually, I think, misleading: fuller of quarrels and debts and love affairs, things common to us all, than of the specific and distinguishing business of authorship. Most modern lives of the poets resemble, indeed, the daily press in their addiction to sensational episodes and their neglect of what is normal. We read in our morning newspaper of seductions, abandonments, and divorces, but of the normal work of Cupid, of the vast average married happiness of the nation, not a word. So it is very often with these lives of authors. Maurois' *Ariel*, for example, which set or helped to set a fashion, tells us quite charmingly all manner of things about Shelley; but the most important thing of all, how and why he was a poet, and how and when he did his work, is hardly touched.

It is the peculiar gift of responsible literary biography that it enables us to see our man twice, once in his writings and again in his life. Do they fit, we ask? And if not, why don't they? The prime example in recent years has been the biography of Wordsworth. A little scandal long suppressed, but at last revealed, has seemed to renovate by its suggestion the whole study of this poet. The pleasure of finding that Wordsworth had a past, that his youth resembled so much less than had been supposed the middle age of other men! The thing itself, the *liaison*, is of quite secondary importance, but it is a link in the tangled chain of interpretation. Every student of Wordsworth has had to look at him afresh, and has found that he was looking at him in a new way. The poet's indignation may be conceived could he have known of these disclosures, and of the knot of researchers who have written books about them. In such matters he was jealous, and as late as 1820 still regarded Boswell's *Life of Johnson* as an ungentlemanly book, an unwarrantable interference with the intimacies of private life. Tennyson later, and Browning, so far at least as their own privacy was concerned, took much the same view. But I am afraid it is useless; the more eminent the writer the less privacy must he expect. The relation between a poet and a reader, says Mr. Garrod, is not, and was never meant to be, the relation, as we call it, between one gentleman and another. It would be at least as true to say that 'a poet is a man who throws a stone at your window (if he is a poet of any power he breaks it). You run to the window, or you pursue him down the street, because you, quite properly, want to know something more about him than the stone. A great poet is not an ordinary occurrence . . . A great poet is a challenge; and he must abide our question. He may, no doubt, claim certain reserves, just as he claims copyright—and perhaps for about the same period. . . .' But, in general, 'we are entitled to all the talk, small and great, about great poets which we can scrape together; with this proviso, that we make a proper use of it: that we can, and do, relate it to the primary fact about them, namely that they *are* great.'

I think this is true, and that a poet is less than most men in a position to object. For poets themselves have never been good at 'suppressing'; indeed it is one of their plainest duties not to suppress. A corresponding candour may fairly be looked for from their biographers. The biographer of a great poet, so long as he knows what he is about, should be as bad at suppressing as the poet himself.

I suppose that biography, whether of authors or of other men, was never better understood, at any rate, than it is to-day. To a more rigorous research, and a much higher degree of candour than was usual even twenty years ago, it has added, not always culpably, the engaging methods of the novel. There will still, no doubt, be family biographies, glossy, high-minded, and unsatisfactory. There will still be examples, though fewer and more furtive, of those bio-graphies which spoke of 'drawing a veil,' and how the poets have suffered from them is too painful a story for this occasion. I can remember our derision as undergraduates over the concluding sentence of a short biography of Marlowe in what was then a standard work, *The History of English Dramatic Literature* by William Adolphus Ward. The sentence was this: 'No comment is needed on such a life with such an end.' It is some measure of our progress not only in literature but in life that to-day no comment would be needed on such a biographer.

In the biographical renaissance of our times a prominent place must be given to the rather belated discovery that the childhood and youth of a writer, and especially of a poet, are an essential part of the biographer's subject. It was a discovery not made by the twentieth century, though we have exploited it. The change of perspective implied was forced upon the attention of the nineteenth century by the precocious lives and early deaths of some of its finest poets. The gospel of it all is in Shelley's *Adonais*, and what is missing in that brief allegory was almost biblically supplied by the *Prelude* of Wordsworth. The biography of poets, and presently biography in general, took a new turn. In the eighteenth century, when the biographical form took shape again in Europe, the biographer, whether of poets or of potentates, hastens always to the grown man. All is adult, all is mature. That every poet must go to school, and to a university if he can, and write boyish verses, and fall in love and out of it, all this to Samuel Johnson, the master biographer of the eighteenth century, seemed a trivial and merely normal introduction to the real experiences and trials of life.

We judge these things differently to-day. We have a craving for beginnings, for the seeds of things, for the flower in the bud. It is now, psychology aiding, almost too amply recognized that in those once unnoticed years of youth and childhood every one of us accumulates by far the most valuable part of the natural riches on which we are to draw for life. On this fresh capital the poet above all men lives, and when it is spent, the man may walk, but the poet is no more. No poet, therefore, who really is a poet, can ever outlive his youth, and it is merely true that all good poets die young.

There is an evident danger, of course, that this discovery may be pushed too far, like the related discovery which has revolutionized our domestic life, the discovery that our children have minds and souls of their own which are entitled to our studious respect. Biography, in its pursuit of origins, runs the risk of becoming morbidly and irrelevantly inquisitive. The lives of some of our poets are already, as I have said, much better known than their works, and their letters more often cited than their poems. Our ears are exercised, not in the still Temple of Urania, but in the buzz and whisper of the House of Fame, and 'even in still lower traffic, the illicit pleasures of the keyhole,' while over all the new psychology casts her darker tinge. These, however, are the shadows of what I must think a beneficent change.

THE ART AND ETHICS OF MODERN BIOGRAPHY

WE live in an age of considerable literary discomfort. In all the higher reaches of our literature, both verse and prose, are old mutterings and rumblings of revolution. Literature in all its branches is to be harmonized, if need be violently, with the modern mind: a mind in itself not especially valuable (that, I think, is hardly claimed by its disillusioned owners), but at any rate *our* mind, and a mind better known, more persistently probed, more diligently analysed, than any mind that ever was. From this tangle of artistic and psychological unrest good things by sheer vitality have emerged, but none more attractive, more timely or provocative, than that agile and sensitive organism which we are now to examine. Here at least is something to consort with, a rebel at once intelligent and gay. If I were asked which class of writers had innovated most successfully in the last ten or twelve years—had evoked most honest thought, provoked most healthy anger, and given most wholesome pleasure—I think that I should be bound to answer, the biographers.

The prince and leader of their race, the master, indeed, of the modern biographers of two continents, was Lytton Strachey. What a talent and intelligence has disappeared with him! What promise of wit unspoken, of books unwritten! We regret his death, and the untimely eclipse of that audacious art. Yet, because it *is* Lytton Strachey, we must not, I remind myself, lament overmuch. Grief, said Dr. Johnson, is a kind of idleness, and so, I should imagine, Strachey thought too. Certainly I have nowhere observed in any of his writings that he respected Death, or reverenced the Dead as such—or Age either. How his eye (if you remember) lights up at a Deathbed, and he celebrated many: it was one of his properties, his opportunities. How he glows with irony at the Victorian drama of Everlastings! Even the frustration of death, even the disappointed hopes of a man suddenly cut off, affect Lytton Strachey like a bungled game or a lost bet. Dr. Arnold, the night before he died, thought of the 'works which, with God's permission,' he would do 'before the night cometh.' Dr. Arnold, Strachey throws in, 'was thinking of his great work on Church and State.' Strachey, you will see, scores doubly. He makes it clear, in the first place, that it would not, in his opinion, have been a 'great work' even if Arnold had lived to write it. And being in the strong historical position of knowing that, Dr. Arnold would never write it, but would die next morning, he twits him again. Dr. Arnold, we are to understand, had lost the rubber. To Age and Decline he is almost invariably pitiless. With what enjoyment, from the wings, he shoos the old men off the stage! Even senility, which befalls the greatest, yields this merciless ironist his characteristic effects.

'When old age actually came, something curious happened. Destiny, having waited very patiently, played a queer trick on Miss Nightingale. The benevolence and public spirit of that long life had only been equalled by its acerbity. Her virtue had dwelt in hardness. . . . And now the sarcastic years brought the proud woman her punishment. She was not to die as she had lived. The sting was to be taken out of her; she was to be made soft; she was to be reduced to compliance and complacency. The change came gradually, but at last it was unmistakable. . . . The thin, angular woman, with her haughty eye and her acid mouth, had vanished; and in her place was the rounded bulky form of a fat old lady, smiling all day long. Then something else became visible. The brain which had been steeled at Scutari was indeed, literally, soft. Senility—an ever more and more amiable senility—descended. Towards the end, consciousness itself grew lost in a roseate haze, and melted into nothingness.'

He adds, as a relish, that this was three years before her death.

Yet his conviction of truth is passionate. He had demonstrated in this portrait, as he believed, the cruelty of a really hard-bitten good woman. Even for the bitter ending there are reasons in art. Strachey above all other biographers, though his imitators aspire to it, had the novelist's power of suggesting the passage of time. He can make it race or stand still as his facts require. If he lingers over her end, the disease itself was lingering. Yet—if I may clumsily borrow his trick of style—why was it that while he wrote this page, and read it softly to himself, a smile not altogether pleasant rested for a moment on his features? And could those be the words that escaped, and no more, his lips—'Euchred, Flo!'?

I have plunged into Strachey because at every point, of the biographers of this generation, whether at home or abroad, I find him, on comparison, the prime artist and innovator. He has been followed, of course, both where he is strong and where he is weak. His method was exemplary. Having found, by whatever instinct, his period, his man, some voluminous person, preferably, if possible a diarist and letter-writer, the subject already of biographers' attentions, the more elaborate the better, he would step daintily down as from some considerable height, pass the person through his mind, with all the documents, and wait, with detached amusement and the utmost patience, to see what came out. No pressure meanwhile must be exerted, of loyalty or friendship, of like or dislike. So far as possible the experiment must be scientific. The biographer, of course, has his creed, his point of view. And what passes through his mind, his mind being what it is, will not come out as it went in. If it should, then no biography. A mistake has been made.

This was his method, and, so far as that goes, it would be hard to find a better.

The great weakness of Strachey, as master and as model, was his lack of what can only be called religion. He has neither gods nor heroes, and with this equipment operates confidently on people who had both. The chance for irony is immense, but the gain to truth more doubtful. It can hardly be supposed that a writer who not only has no religion of his own, but is honestly incapable of understanding it in others, should be successful as a biographer of a religious man. His group of eminent Victorians—Manning, Arnold, and Gordon especially—present him at every turn with this insuperable difficulty. But there they were, irresistibly tempting, and he could not leave them alone. The result was to suggest that he chose and to some extent succeeded with his subjects because he disliked them, and it has been laughable to see the hurry-scurry of biographers to act on this hint. I prefer myself the hero-worship of Boswell and the tenderness of Lockhart to this imitative and manufactured peevishness, and am handsomely confirmed in my preference by their respective products. The present fluttering activity of these writers of Lives in which disparagement of great men is adopted by a method reminds me of some verses of Tom Moore. Biography, it would appear, was in 1828 almost as popular a trade as it is now:

> Next week will be published (as 'Lives' are the rage)
>   The whole reminiscences, wondrous and strange,
> Of a small puppy dog that lived once in the cage
>   Of the late noble lion at Exeter 'Change.
>
> How that animal eats, how he snores, how he drinks,
>   Is all noted down by this Boswell so small,
> And 'tis plain from each sentence the puppy dog thinks,
>   That the lion was no such great thing after all.
>
> 'Tis indeed as good fun as a cynic could ask
>   To see how this cockney-bred setter of rabbits
> Takes gravely the Lord of the Forest to task
>   And judges of lions by puppy dog habits.

Eminent Victorians, though not the best of Strachey's books, will always historically be the most important; for it was there that he first declared himself, and started a movement. No book was ever better timed. Coming when it did, in the last six months of the War, it was still fresh when the young men returned, and became at once the exhilarating text-book of their discontent. Their half-articulate grudge against their Victorian elders found solace and mirth in its polite, its so infinitely polite damnation. Even the older generation enjoyed the fun, at least the free minds among them, and cheered Strachey on. 'Don't worry if you're abused,' Sir Walter Raleigh wrote to him; 'the noise is produced by the din you make.' The book was a counterblast. 'If you go for Samuel Smiles, he has friends who go for you. But he can't hurt you. We want your method,' he went on, 'for some stately Victorians who have waited long for it. First the great Panjandrum—Victoria Herself. This is obvious. . . . Next, Jowett! I am keenest about this. Remember no Don has ever been properly done, full-length. . . . Then Tennyson. (I believe, in the main, he will be let off.) I also want Dizzy. It's really wicked of you to leave those stout volumes alone, when you could put the gist of them within reach of us.' His wish has been answered, though not entirely by Strachey, who matured his works. Victoria he did; Tennyson has been rehandled; and the stout volumes of Mr. Buckle's *Disraeli* have been plundered in the authentic Stracheyan manner for the biographical nosegay of M. Maurois. Only Jowett awaits a psychologist who can also write.

'Every hero becomes a bore at last,' said Emerson, and the Victorian idols were tottering before Strachey put out his hand. In that campaign he is the last of the captains. His creed, on the other hand, was novel. He is the first of our biographers to proclaim himself explicitly a naturalist— which is what his lusty follower Ludwig also calls himself— a biological fisher in the sea of history. His Preface to *Eminent Victorians* is still the best pronouncement on the modern manner of biography, on its relation to History and its independence as an Art. He begins by giving up the history of the Victorian age. It will never be written, because we know too much about it:

'For ignorance is the first requisite of the historian— ignorance which simplifies and clarifies, which selects and omits, with a placid perfection unattainable by the highest art. Concerning the Age which has just passed, our fathers and our grandfathers have poured forth and accumulated so vast a quantity of information that the industry of a Ranke would be submerged by it, and the perspicacity of a Gibbon would quail before it. It is not by the direct method of a scrupulous narration that the explorer of the past can hope to depict that singular epoch. If he is wise, he will adopt a subtler strategy. He will attack his subject in unexpected places; he will fall upon the flank, or the rear; he will shoot a sudden, revealing searchlight into obscure recesses, hitherto undivined. He will row out over that great ocean of material, and lower down into it, here and there, a little bucket, which will bring up to the light of day some characteristic specimen, from those far depths, to be examined with a careful curiosity. Guided by these considerations, I have written the ensuing studies.'

So much for Victorian history, which only biography can rescue from its embarrassment. But what of Biography itself, that neglected art, for 'human beings are too important to be treated as mere symptoms of the past. They have a value which is independent of any temporal processes—which is eternal, and must be felt for its own sake.' The art of biography had fallen on evil times in England. We had had, it was true, a few masterpieces, but we had never had, like the French, a great biographical tradition. . . . With us, the most delicate and humane of all the branches of the art of writing had been relegated to the journeymen of letters; we did not reflect that it was perhaps as difficult to write a good life as to live one. Those two fat volumes, with which it was our custom to commemorate the dead—who did not know them, with their ill-digested masses of material, their slipshod style, their tone of tedious panegyric, their lamentable lack of selection, of detachment, of design? They were as familiar as the cortege of the undertaker, and wore the same air of slow, funereal barbarism. One was tempted to suppose, of some of them, that they were composed by that functionary, as the final item of his job.

'The studies in this book,' Lytton Strachey goes on, 'are indebted, in more ways than one, to such works—works, which certainly deserve the name of Standard Biographies. For they have provided me not only with much indispensable information, but with something even more precious—an example. How many lessons are to be learnt from them! But it is hardly necessary to particularize. To preserve, for instance, a becoming brevity—a brevity which excludes everything that is redundant and nothing that is significant —that, surely, is the first duty of the biographer. The second, no less surely, is to maintain his own freedom of spirit. It is not his business to be complimentary; it is his business to lay bare the facts of the case, as he understands them.'

This is a brave ideal, and was not reached without struggle. Froude, with all his faults, had fought that battle, for the right to be uncomplimentary, and to have the freedom of his own mind. Even Lockhart, because he wrote frankly, was accused of a treacherous attempt to dishero Scott. Rogers the poet could only suppose that he disliked him. Every biographer who told the truth had his particular skirmish; even the Boswellian question, the reporting of conversation, took nearly a century to resolve. Lockhart went so far as to protest against the fidelity of several literary gentlemen who had forwarded to him private lucubrations of theirs, designed to Boswellize Scott. His reasons, or one of them, was not always sufficiently present to the mind of Strachey, as he reached out for telling anecdotes, and is indeed too commonly ignored in biographies of all kinds. Lockhart says:

'To report conversations fairly, it is a necessary prerequisite that we should be completely familiar with all the interlocutors, and understand thoroughly all their minutest relations, and points of common knowledge and common feeling, with each other. He who does not, must be perpetually in danger of misinterpreting sportive allusions into serious statement; and the man who was only recalling by some jocular phrase or half-phrase, to an old companion, some trivial reminiscence of their boyhood or youth, may be represented as expressing, upon some person or incident casually tabled, an opinion which he had never framed, or if he had, would never have given words to in any mixed assemblage—not even among what the world calls "friends" at his own board. In proportion as a man is witty and humorous, there will always be about him and his a widening maze and wilderness of cues and catchwords, which the uninitiated will, if they are bold enough to try interpretation, construe, ever and anon, egregiously amiss—not seldom into arrant falsity. For this one reason, to say nothing of many others, I consider no man justified in journalizing what he sees and hears in a domestic circle where he is not thoroughly at home; and I think there are still higher and better reasons why he should not do so where he is.'

Tennyson was of the same mind, and praised 'unrecording friends.' As he put it, in a not very characteristic couplet:

> While I live, the Owls;
> When I die, the Ghouls.

An unhelpful world for the biographer.

Here also, Strachey inherited an ease which he did not make. I say nothing of earlier experiments, but think it proper to claim, in the biographical innovations of the present century, a place of some importance for the late Sir Edmund Gosse. He even preceded Strachey in the most important of his enterprises, and under much more difficult conditions. In 1901, three months after her death, there appeared from his pen in the April *Quarterly* an article on Queen Victoria. 'No idea of the sensation it created,' says Mr. Charteris, Sir Edmund's biographer, 'can be formed without recapturing the state of the public mind at the time.' To-day the article reads as a blameless and successful attempt to estimate some of the personal qualities of the Queen. In April, 1901, the attempt hardly escaped the charge of sacrilege. . . . More than twenty years later Gosse, in reviewing the Life of Queen Victoria by Lytton Strachey, reminded his readers of the feeling which found expression at the time:

'Her phantom took divine proportions; she was clothed with the most extravagant and the most incongruous attributes, and anyone who endeavoured, in however respectful and even affectionate terms, to separate the fabulous from the historic elements, and reduce the vast idol to human proportions, was regarded as libellous and cruel.'

'Had Gosse,' says Charteris, 'been detected in the act of cutting a caper at the august lady's memorable funeral, he could hardly have earned more reprobation. . . . And yet in reality he had rendered a service to the memory of the Queen; he had arrested the growth of a myth, it is true, but he had replaced it by the delineation of an extremely human and sovereign woman. . . . With touches of decorous and scarcely perceptible irony he put into more exact perspective the extravagant titles with which she had been invested by the popular imagination. While detracting nothing from the basic greatness of her character, he succeeded in evoking a portrait differing little from the most modern delineations of which the Queen has been the subject.'

A still more daring act of biographical innovation must be recorded: the publication in 1907 of Gosse's famous *Father and Son*. It commanded attention for two reasons: as a work of literature it was of the highest excellence; it was also, biographically, of a searching and persistent candour which would have been startling in any biography and seemed even shocking when the biography was of a father by his son. Gosse, in his essay on Lytton Strachey's *Eminent Victorians*, declares that 'In this country the majority have always enjoyed seeing noses knocked off statues.' It is forgivable that the first readers of *Father and Son* should have supposed it to be a signal example of this process, with the added piquancy, as Charteris remarks, that it was the features of a father which were being mutilated. 'The author of this book,' said a reviewer in *The Times Literary Supplement*, 'has no doubt settled it with his conscience how far in the interests of popular edification and amusement it is legitimate to expose the weaknesses and inconsistencies of a good man who is also one's father.' 'To a later generation,' Charteris maintains, 'this criticism seems whimsical and irrelevant. It reads like the last splutter of the Old Guard, still standing for panegyric rather than truth as the staple of biography.' Gosse claimed that the book was a tribute to his father, an extraordinary man. 'It is not,' he wrote 'of the same order as the lying epitaphs in churchyards, but I hope it is something better: an exact portrait of a good and even great man whose character was too powerful not to have its disconcerting sides.' Gosse, though at first shocked at the undermining of his dear Victorians, was one of the first to welcome Strachey's talent. I now place him among Strachey's ancestors.

Some five or six years ago Emil Ludwig, the somewhat muscular Strachey of Germany, gave his views on historical portraiture and the new biography. He noted, as others have done, that after a period in which biography attempted to define man in terms of descent and breeding, of heredity and environment, we are entered now upon an era not much moved by the Darwinian conception.

'Once again' [he says] 'we turn our attention to the personality *per se*, the personality almost devoid of temporal processes, considering . . . its vital forces, the restless fluid of its emotions, and the balance between its impulse towards action and its repression through precept. Whereas our fathers asked, "How did the man harmonize with his world?" our first question is, "Does he harmonize with himself?" Questions of success and responsibility have been shifted from the environment back to the individual, and the analysis which was formerly expended on the milieu now seeks to penetrate within. The new interest is biological. The typical biographer of to-day is first of all a psychologist, and is much nearer to the biologist than to the historian. . . . His problem remains constant: it is the discovery of a human soul.'

I see no reason why this problem should defeat him, but I see also that the nearer he approaches the biologist the further he will recede from literature. We shall have biography specialists—indeed Ludwig talks of them—and then the game for me is lost. Fortunately the new biographers are dependent on yet other biographers for their material in those much derided two volumes in octavo. If the worse comes to the worst, I shall line my shelves with them.

I spoke of Lockhart, whom I am not ashamed to own as my favourite among biographers. There is a passage in one of his letters which should be a comfort to all writers of Lives and a caution to all readers of them. He is writing of the reception of his Life of Scott. 'The criticisms,' he says, 'were, of course, contradictory. The book was too cheap; it was too dear; it was too long; it was too short; it told too much; it did not tell enough; Sir Walter was too much glorified; Sir Walter was traduced.'

In other words, a perfect Biography.

MORGANN ON FALSTAFF [1]

WHAT man it was who first suggested to a publisher that other centuries than his own should have their chance of reading Morgann we do not know, but whoever he was, we think well of him and honour his memory. It was in 1777 that the Essay first appeared, and won the praise of 'ingenuity' from the cognoscenti; but nothing could overcome the repugnance of its author to a second edition. He had published once with reluctance, and he would do no more. Twenty-five years later Morgann died, but it was not until 1820 that the Essay appeared again, with its author's name; the brief moment of interest (or was it hope?) which inspired the third issue of 1825 passed and left no trace; and from then until 1903, when Mr. Nichol Smith included it in his *Eighteenth Century Essays on Shakespeare*, it sank almost wholly out of sight, overwhelmed in the romantic deluge which, more than any other Shakespearian pronouncement of the eighteenth century, it had foreseen and invited. Since that date, many who had only heard of the Essay have come to know it; and when a man comes to know a thing like this, he tells his friends; but still there was no single book, no book called Morgann's, which one could buy on an afternoon. That want is now supplied; and Mr. Gill, in helping to supply it, has testified more vividly than was to be expected how great was the need, for he is ignorant of the existence of Mr. Nichol Smith's edition, though it is a model of editing, and believes his own, which is the fifth edition, to be the fourth. But these are niceties. The publishers and the public, conspiring together, will soon confound these numerals. There will be many editions of

---

[1] A review of *Morgann's Essay on the Dramatic Character of Sir John Falstaff*, edited by W. A. Gill. Reprinted from *The Times Literary Supplement*, 15th November 1912.

Morgann's Essay before the century is out, though none, perhaps, more agreeable than the fifth.

There is always a reason for neglect, and it is generally a good reason; the chief delinquent in this case was Morgann himself. He was an incorrigible amateur; the disease of anonymity had undone him. Though he was at one time an Under-Secretary of State, and was employed on various missions on American affairs at a time when no other affairs were so important, though he lived and died in London, went everywhere, and knew every one, he has left fewer records than could have been thought possible of his seventy-six years of life. Every active episode in his career is followed by a blank which no editor has yet succeeded in filling. It is possible, of course, that there is nothing to record; he may have done nothing; but he must have talked, at least, and seen his friends. As it is, we know him only in general terms, as a cultivated man of affairs and private lover of human character and speculation (the ideal reader of Shakespeare); as one who read, not for gain or show, but for his private recreation, and wrote, for the most part, to the same end; interested in public questions and accepting such responsibility as the great might thrust upon him, but jealous of his freedom and shy of officialdom, preferring to be consulted rather than employed; above all, a bachelor of leisure, fond of children and talk. The *post obit* halo of a literary name had no attractions for him compared to the inconvenience of appearing in so self-conscious and public a character as that of author; he was not inclined to solicit for his private amusements the approval of mankind. It was his good or bad fortune to be neither poor nor ambitious; and it is generally admitted by that acuter portion of the race which leaves writing to others that to be successful a writer should be both, with this addendum, that, as the first so often makes the second unnecessary, it is on that account the more necessary quality of the two. Sinecures and pensions, however, and the consideration of his friends supplied all Morgann's wants; and it would seem that for the greater part of his life he was content to live. Heaven, he had to confess it, acting in this as in all things for the best, had laid upon him the unaccountable burden of scribbling. He was a scribbler, it was useless to deny it; but yet he saw no reason in nature why the world should be forced to weigh his burden, or think itself or him either the better or the worse for it; it was enough that the burden was his, and that he could be relieved of it when he chose. His writings, when they appeared at all, appeared without his name; the rest were destroyed at his death—to the great loss, as we must think, of criticism and letters. For he had a free mind, as his Essay shows, and brave notions, and when the fit was on him could strum the chords of the sensuous understanding (the romancer's guitar) better than many a romantic critic who lived after him, was poor, and made a name.

But the Essay? The masterpiece? Like so many good things, it began in a jest. He undertook for a wager to prove that Falstaff was 'not intended to be shown as a Coward,' and to publish the proof. The result was the Essay on Falstaff, written 'in a very short time,' and with some subsequent revision published three years later. It is addressed to readers as 'unengaged' as himself, and seems at first sight to pretend to nothing more than a whimsical vindication of Falstaff from the calumniations of the age—for in 'this great article' of Falstaff's cowardice the age was agreed. What happened was what was bound to happen, and what Morgann foresaw. We are the slaves of grimace. In spite of his repeated warnings—'Falstaff is the word only, Shakespeare is the theme'— the book was skimmed and thrown aside as a *jeu d'esprit*, a thing of cap and bells, and the critics went back to their broadcloth. The opportunity of making amends which a second edition might have given was sternly withheld, so that when Hazlitt printed his 'Characters of Shakespeare' forty years later he could recollect only two English writers (one of whom he misnames) who professed to do at all what he was sure he had done well; for a third name he had to call upon the hosts of Germany. Morgann had escaped him, to his loss; nor is there any sign that he or any other of the greater Romantics took advantage of the opportunity presented to them in 1820 and 1825 of hearing a gentleman of the eighteenth century speak to them on their favourite subject with an insight and eloquence equal to their own. Had Hazlitt read Morgann it is safe to say that we should have heard a good deal less about the wonderful discoveries of Schlegel.

For Morgann is not only an innovator; he is a conscious and explicit innovator; he takes risks. 'The whole is a mere Experiment,' he says, 'and the writer considers it as such. It may have the advantages, but it is likewise attended with all the difficulties and dangers of Novelty.' And more explicitly, as he goes on:

> The reader will not need to be told that this Inquiry will resolve itself into a Critique on the genius, the arts, and the conduct of Shakespeare: For what is Falstaff, what Lear, what Hamlet, or Othello, but different modifications of Shakespeare's thought? It is true that this Inquiry is narrowed almost to a single point: But general criticism is as uninstructive as it is easy: Shakespeare deserves to be considered in detail—a task hitherto unattempted.

It soon becomes plain that, whatever Eastcheap and Gadshill and Shrewsbury may hold out for us, they are not the sole or even the principal objects of our journey; we are to deal with the fundamentals of dramatic art.

It is easy to see how Morgann was led on. The first thing that strikes us when we reflect upon a character like Falstaff's is the incongruity of it, and the corresponding incongruity between our judgment and our feelings. 'No part whatever of his character seems to be fully settled in our minds.' The understanding, if we use it at all, convicts him of cowardice and vice—to no effect, for our impressions acquit him of any of the consequences. A vicious coward, however amusing at the time, should be condemned on reflection: but this is not our feeling of Falstaff's character. 'When he has ceased to amuse us we feel no emotions of disgust.' When Parolles and Bobadil are detected and exposed they pass out, their hold is lost; and not only when they are exposed, but the first time they are exposed. But Falstaff is continually detected

and exposed, and so far are we from ceasing to be interested
in his career that all we wish and pray for, all that his friends
seem to live for in their leisure, is the next exposure. After
every fall he is still the same. 'We see him rise again like a
boy from play, and run another race with as little dishonour
as before.' What are we to say to this? That there is a *real*
character of Falstaff, and an *apparent* one, and that by some
stealth of art or nature the first is obscured from every part
of us except our feelings, which fly out to what the understanding cannot see. Are we, then, the fools of Nature, or of
Shakespeare, or of both? Of both, cries Morgann, for Shakespeare is Nature. We are face to face with the fundamental
problem of imaginative drama, the presentation, within the
harmony of art, of those living incongruities of nature without
which humour is a name and all character a mask. In the
subtle management by which the dramatist, intent on impression and impression only, eludes the approaches of the
disintegrating understanding and steals upon the comprehensive passions of the soul, Morgann believed that Shakespeare had surpassed not only all other dramatists but even
the conceived capacities of man.

> The characters of every drama [he says] must indeed be
> grouped; but in the groups of other poets the parts which are
> not seen do not in fact exist. But there is a certain roundness
> and integrity in the forms of Shakespeare. . . . Very frequently,
> when no particular point presses, he boldly makes a character
> act and speak from those parts of the composition which are
> *inferred* only, and not distinctly shown. This produces a wonder-
> ful effect; it seems to carry us beyond the poet to nature itself
> . . . and this is in reality that art in Shakespeare which, being
> withdrawn from our notice, we more emphatically call *nature*.
> A felt propriety and truth from causes unseen, I take to be the
> highest point of poetic composition. If the characters of Shake-
> speare are thus *whole*, and, as it were, original, while those of
> almost all other writers are mere imitation, it may be fit to con-
> sider them rather as historic than dramatic beings; and,
> when occasion requires, to account for their conduct from the
> *whole* of character, from general principles, from latent motives,
> and from policies not avowed.

Here, in language which could not easily be surpassed, is the whole creed of the romantic Shakespearians. It is salutary to remember that when it was written Coleridge was still in frocks and Hazlitt not yet born. It has this advantage, also, over their pronouncements, that it affects no absolute break with the past; it stands in the great critical tradition of its century, the last stage of a structure to which Dryden, Pope, and Johnson had all contributed. Even the language is the same, but it is used in a new way. The comparison of Shakespeare to nature, the oldest thing in Shakespearian criticism, has here for the first time a genuine and vital meaning.

The passage we have quoted is one of a series of three, the finest in the Essay. They are a succession of outbursts, the cries of a romantic awakening to the light. He is weary of the folly and short-sightedness of critics, and calls aloud for 'some new Stagyrite' who will 'enter into the inward soul' of Shakespeare's works. As for the pedants and detractors,

> When the hand of time shall have brushed off his present Editors and Commentators, and the very name of Voltaire, and even the memory of the language in which he has written, shall be no more, the Apalachian mountains, the banks of the Ohio, and the plains of Sciota shall resound with the accents of this barbarian. In his native tongue he shall roll the genuine passions of nature; nor shall the griefs of Lear be alleviated, or the charms and wit of Rosalind be abated by time. There is, indeed, nothing perishable about him, except that very learning which he is said so much to want. . . . Milton and he will carry the decayed remnants and fripperies of antient mythology into more distant ages than they are by their own force entitled to extend, and the *Metamorphoses* of Ovid, upheld by them, lay in a new claim to unmerited immortality.

This is eloquence, and when Morgann is eloquent he does not leave things as he found them; but it is far surpassed by the statement which follows, on the genius of Shakespeare: the most eloquent and comprehensive in the book. It is the last of our three passages, and the best, and it shall be left to the reader, along with the analysis of magic, the defence of Shakespeare's puns, and the discourse on the allied natures of Tragedy and Comedy. There is no timidity in Morgann; he is gallant, like his country; and at every point, when he has to do with poetry, he speaks with the accent of the generation which followed his own. The account of his illumination and conversion from the superstition of the Rules would have delighted Coleridge.

> Convinced, I see that a more compendious nature may be obtained; a nature of *effects* only, to which neither the relations of place nor continuity of time are always essential. Nature, condescending to the faculties and apprehensions, of man, has drawn through human life a regular chain of visible causes and effects: but Poetry delights in surprise, conceals her steps, seizes at once upon the heart, and obtains the Sublime of things without betraying the rounds of her ascent. True Poesy is *magic*, not *nature*; an effect from causes hidden or unknown. To the Magician [he goes on, speaking of Shakespeare] I prescribe no laws; his law and his power are one; his power is his law.

It is a noble gospel of Freedom and Romance to come from a Civil Servant turned fifty in the year 1777. Students of national psychology may see in it a pertinent example of that 'growth outside the law' which is so remarkable a feature of our English institutions. A little company of sympathetic Berkshire squires and parsons, meeting in their spare time in the latter years of the same century, revolutionize the problem of wages in England; Maurice Morgann, in one of his intervals of ease, seated in his armchair, drafts the manifesto of the romantic revolution in Shakespearian study. The only defect of it is Romantic too: its unconscious ingratitude. The one man in that age who could have 'convinced' Morgann was Johnson, whose Preface decided for ever in England the question of the Rules and of Tragi-Comedy; decided it, too, on grounds so valid and universal that the French Romantics, when they came to fight their battle, were perfectly happy to repeat his arguments. It made everything else possible. When Victor Hugo began to write, he found these old giants of the Rules and Tragi-Comedy the first in his path. When Coleridge and Hazlitt began to write, they found these giants dead by the way, and never asked who killed them. Morgann must have known, and should have told.

We have said little about the character of Falstaff, though most of the book is occupied with it. The chief value of the Essay, as Morgann insists, is to be found in the generous speculations to which Falstaff points the way. It must be confessed, also, that the arrangement is not tidy. The wager, the hasty writing and revision have had their effect; it is a scene of admirable disorder. For all that, Falstaff bestrides it like a Colossus. Every scrap of evidence on the fat fellow's life is produced and inspected, and always the slighter the evidence the more probable and buoyant seems the inference. Morgann is very good to Falstaff on the evidence: furnishes him with a family crest on the strength of the ring, and with rooms in Town (because it is 'clear from the circumstances of the arrest that he did not lodge at the tavern'): gives him a regular table for the sake of Master Gower, and the pension besides, not in prospect but in actuality, *now*: even holds out a hint of 'some funds which are not brought immediately under our notice,' and goes so far as to believe that the ring was really gold (in the main), though he will not engage himself for the bonds. Scoggon, too, the jester, must be 'some boisterous fencer,' because young Falstaff broke his head. But even in all this multiplicity of detail—which, it should be remembered, was as new in such subjects as the principles we have discussed—even here Morgann never misses a chance of speculation. We are reminded of his friend Cooke's account of his conversation, which Mr. Gill quotes:

> His creative fancy branched upon such an infinite variety of views as made it sometimes difficult for him to settle upon the close point, but when he gained that point (*which he generally did*) with what eloquence and perspicuity did he support it!

Morgann always comes back to Falstaff's courage in the end, and always with some new light drawn from the whole of character. Of the two kinds of courage open to man, constitutional courage and the courage that is founded on principle, Falstaff, he proves, has the first; it is in the whole carriage of the man—his gaiety and ease in every situation. The second he is without, because he chose to reject the principle. He is 'a kind of military freethinker,' with 'too much wit for a hero.' This idea of Falstaff as the old soldier is fruitful. It explains many of his ways, and he is treated as an old soldier by every one but his cronies, Hal and Poins. See him on Shrewsbury Field; he is as much at home as First Grave-digger in his yard, and has the same jocular realism about his trade. 'Custom hath made it in him a property of easiness.' His rejection of the rigid principle of honour is thus professionally explained. He speaks of grinning Honour as he does because he had so often seen it grin, on Honour's truckle-bed, that is to say, in the ditch after a battle. It is the philosophy of the mercenary or professional soldier; of Captain Dugald Dalgetty and all his friends. It turns their practice into theory. Such a theory, it is obvious, makes good soldiers but bad heroes, which is one way of showing up war. It is the duty of the professional, whether he be a soldier or a footballer, to spare himself 'when he sees reason.' He cannot afford to compress all life into a moment and be the hero; he has to go on as usual to-morrow. Looked at in this way, Falstaff's dissection of Honour becomes doubly natural. It is not only natural to a mind which saw all things in ridiculous lights; it is nature itself when such a man happens to be also an old campaigner. Falstaff, of course, with that rotundity of mind and body which is the source of all his mirth, goes over the heads of the Dalgettys as far as his endowments exceed theirs. He extends his philosophy beyond the field of battle to all the transactions of human existence. He spares himself everywhere like a professional, for his profession is nothing less than life.

There are many other speculations in Morgann. But there is no end to the breeding of ideas in such a mind as his; what he wants is readers to work them out. They might add to their investigations an inquiry into the alleged harmony or proportion between corpulence and vice, or, again, between a man's waist and his wit. On the first problem, speaking with the authority of one who carried all the evidence in his person, Falstaff has pronounced in terms which no man of true feeling was ever known to resist, and which theology itself can scarcely refuse: 'I have more flesh than another man, and therefore more frailty.' We refer the student to this position, and for illustration of it to the (still unpublished!) list in the MS. commonplace book of Jasper Fyloll, a Dominican, of Syon Monastery, in the reign of Henry VIII: *Hii sunt quorum iniquitas ex adipe procedit.* On both themes, Morgann would have done well; they were, no doubt, among the 'many pressing considerations' which he 'resisted.' In the meantime, to raise the wind of his fame, some title is wanted which posterity may use in the descriptive headings of its text-books. We are to express much genius, much neglect, and some contributory negligence. Let us call Morgann the Blake of Shakespearian criticism, and await results.

SIR WALTER RALEGH

ON 24th October, 300 years ago, Sir Walter Ralegh, after many examinations and interrogatories, awaiting judgment in the Tower, was brought before the Council at Whitehall and informed of his approaching end. He asked that he might be beheaded and not hanged, and so much was allowed. He was now in his sixty-sixth year, and in spite of his fourteen years' confinement and the fevers and tragedies of his Guiana voyage, still vigorous and unbroken, still rebuking, by a certain Elizabethan splendour which he could not lose, the meaner world of James. His contemporaries could not think of him as old; nor, indeed, can we. Four days later the warrant was signed and sentence pronounced. Even yet there was hope, though for his part he had none. The Queen pleaded for him; his friends spoke for him—for he still had friends: but the King was stubborn and morose. On Thursday, 29th October, in Old Palace-yard, Westminster, Ralegh ended on the scaffold his brilliant and tempestuous life, thanking God that 'He had sent him to die in the light, and not in darkness.' Both then and on the previous day he was very cheerful, so that the good Dean of Westminster 'wondered at him,' and his friends begged him not to 'carry it with too much bravery,' lest his enemies should be incensed; he was 'the most fearless of death,' said the Dean, 'that ever was known, and the most resolute and confident.' On the 28th his friends took leave of him at the Gate-house, where he was to spend the night; he said good-bye to 'dear Bess,' his wife; and for the rest of the day was occupied with his thoughts. When the morning came, a great multitude had assembled in front of the Parliament House. Ralegh had feared that there might not be room for his friends: 'I do not know what you may do for a place. For my part, I am sure of one.' He ate his breakfast heartily, and smoked his pipe, making no more of death than if he had been to take a journey. He received the Communion, and was confident of persuading the world that he died an innocent man. There was a fire burning beside the scaffold when he came to it, for the morning was cold and raw; but he would not use it, being in haste to be gone. He saluted his acquaintance, and, proclamation being made, delivered that speech of which a report has come down to us, clearing, as he could, the charges of his enemies and declaring before God his unbroken loyalty to the Crown and to the fortunes of England.

'And now,' he said, 'I entreat you all to join with me in prayer to that great God of Heaven whom I have grievously offended, being a man full of all vanity, and have lived a sinful life in such callings as have been most inducing to it; for I have been a soldier, a sailor, and a courtier.' And 'so,' he ended, 'I take my leave of you all. . . . I have a long journey to take, and must bid the company farewell.'

The ironical formalities of the scaffold went forward. He refused to be blindfolded, and signalled with his hand when he was ready. The executioner hesitated till Ralegh admonished him, and then struck twice. A shudder passed through the crowd, and as the head was shown there was muttering and tears. He had desired, when he lay at Winchester expecting death fifteen years before, that he might be buried either at Sherborne, if his estate there should endure, or 'in Exeter Church by my father and mother'; but it seems that the quickest way was thought the best. His body was conveyed from the scaffold to St. Margaret's Church and there buried in the chancel; not until long afterwards did any record or memorial exist beyond the entry of his name in the burial register. This reproach, by the private action of some English and American citizens who knew the history of their country, has since been removed. It was never, in any case, an index of the truth.

The first claim to possession in the greatness of Ralegh lies, and must always lie, with his county of Devon, where about the year 1552, in the parish of East Budleigh, he was born, a younger son of an honourable West Country family somewhat fallen in fortune. Of his boyhood we know nothing but by tradition: that he was fond of the sea and of sailors, and would read eagerly such books of voyages as came his way. He inherited a handsome body, and a restless, stirring, and independent character, good equipment for a younger son; from his mother, 'a woman of noble wit,' something perhaps of that grace of mind which so well became him; his genius and ambitions were his own. His family was notable for Protestantism at a time when to be a Protestant needed courage; and this temper he retained and confirmed in manhood in the wars of France and Spain. Of his education little is known. 'Not to name the school or the masters of men illustrious for literature,' says Dr. Johnson, 'is a kind of historical fraud, by which honest fame is injuriously diminished.' We know, however, neither his masters nor his school: a defect the less regrettable in the biography of a man who was to prove illustrious for so much else. That he was at some time before his seventeenth year a commoner of Oriel College, Oxford; that he became 'the ornament of the juniors,' and left a reputation for scholarship and wit: this indeed is known; but when we have added from gossip Aubrey that he borrowed a gown of one T. Child and never returned it, we have exhausted the chronicle. The undergraduate was already burning to be a man. The lines are known in which Panthino reproaches a father:

> He wonder'd that your lordship
> Would suffer him to spend his youth at home,
> While other men, of slender reputation,
> Put forth their sons to seek preferment out:
> Some to the wars, to try their fortune there;
> Some to discover islands far away;
> Some to the studious universities.

The father in the end sends his son to Court. Such a catalogue would have been no news to young Ralegh; he had its items by heart, and so true an Elizabethan was he that by the age of twenty-six he had run through them all. Young men need friends, and he was by no means friendless. His

family, though reduced, had many connexions in the West
Country, where cousinship is understood. He counted Gren-
villes, Careys, Drakes, Gilberts, and Champernouns among
his kinsmen, and when he went to fight the Leaguers in
France—*admodum adolescens*, says Camden, *jam primum fatis
monstratus*—it was with a troop of West Country gentlemen
volunteers, commanded by a Champernoun, that he first
saw service. He was absent from England six years, but
except for a sentence or two in his 'History,' where he speaks
as an eye-witness of the retreat after Moncontour, and of
hunting Catholics among the hill-caves of Languedoc, the
haze which covers his childhood covers these years also. On
his return to England the haze lightens. Ralegh had ever the
art of making the best of his surroundings. He needed a club,
and in 1575 he was admitted a student of the Middle Temple.
He desired to feel the pulse of things, and the Inns of Court
were then the geographical and intellectual centre of London.
He aspired to be a courtier, and to be a Templar was already
half-way to Whitehall. His assertions in later life that he had
read no law, which have been held to invalidate his footing
in the Temple, only prove how well he chose his club. He
wrote verses, talked projects, played the gallant, and enjoyed
the town. He even appeared in print. In 1576 Gascoigne's
Steel Glass came out with commendatory verses by 'Walter
Rawely of the Middle Temple,' verses which already in
some of their lines have the very turn and style of Ralegh,
a certain proud terseness and melancholy scorn:

> For whoso reaps renown above the rest,
> With heaps of hate shall surely be opprest.

He had now been at home two years, and grew restless
once more. In 1577 he was off to serve against the Spaniards
in the Low Countries, where his half-brother, Sir Humphrey
Gilbert, commanded one of the English regiments. The sea
claimed him, and next year he sailed with Gilbert on his first
and less unfortunate expedition to Newfoundland. He made
acquaintance at Court. But it was not until his twenty-
eighth year that, on Gilbert's recommendation, he obtained

his first employment in the Queen's service, as a captain of foot with the forces in Ireland. To this half-brother, thirteen years his senior, Ralegh owed at this period much of the practical direction of his mind. He was a notable, warm, high-handed man, bold and inventive; an experienced soldier and speculative navigator, and a patriot who believed that man

> not worthy to live at all who for fear of danger or death shunneth his country's service or his own honour, since death is inevitable and the fame of virtue immortal.

He had schemes for the English empire of the sea; had projected a discovery of the North-West Passage; and dreamed of the occupation, in the Northern parts of America, of territories for the Queen. His lodging at Limehouse, where he sat among his maps and instruments, was at this time a resort of voyagers and venturers; Frobisher and Davis were partners in his researches, and Ralegh, we may be sure, the aptest of learners. The Royal Charter of 1578, by which Gilbert was empowered, for six years, to discover and inhabit vacant heathen lands, and which led him to repeat, in 1583, at the cost of his life, his colonizing expedition to Newfoundland, descended as by inheritance to the younger man whom he had helped to form. On 25th March 1584, a significant date in the history of the New World and of the Old, Walter Ralegh, now in the first stages of his greatness and high in favour with the Queen, obtained a new Charter of discovery and colonization in place of the old. The country on which he had set his heart was that which lies along the Middle Atlantic from what is now Maine to the north of Florida, and with his fervent and practical imagination he saw it already peopled and rivalling in its fruits the Spanish Empire of the Gulf. Five weeks later two ships, under Captains Amadas and Barlowe, his 'servants,' set sail for the new territory, and on 13th July landed on the island of Wokoken, off the North Carolina coast, where they formally proclaimed the sovereignty of the Queen and their master's possession. The whole island was named, it is said by Elizabeth herself, Virginia, and Ralegh had a seal made with the motto

Walteri Ralegh, Militis, Domini et Gubernatoris Virginiae propria insignia, 1584, *amore et virtute.* He was to send many more expeditions to Virginia before his fortunes fell; to lose all, and still hope. It is enough to record, at this moment in his life, the piety of his first great enterprise, his promptitude of execution, and the generosity of his hopes.

The arrival of Ralegh at Court and his first meeting with the Queen—the story of the plush cloak and the puddle—have passed into the substance of English legend. Scott has immortalized a scene which Fuller, nearly three generations after date, was the first to record. The historians, who deny themselves this scene, have been less happy in explaining the lightning promotion of this ill-paid and little-known captain of foot to his place in Elizabeth's regard. He arrives with dispatches one day in December, 1581, from rebel-hunting in Munster, his commission expired and his company disbanded, and in six weeks is acting as the personal agent of the Queen, writing her letters, escorting envoys, and breathing like a native the inner air of the Court! The Queen, it is true, loved a martial man, and Ralegh had served well in Ireland; he spoke boldly and with knowledge about Irish affairs, and for this he was valued; but when she set her mark upon him she saw, with the sensibility of a woman, much more than this. She saw a young man, infinitely gifted in mind and body, eager for service and burning for the light, with the temper of a soldier, the vision of a sailor, and the heart of a poet. She could not afford to lose him, this fisher, as Hatton called her, 'for men's souls.' And so he remained, at some expense to his freedom, and was liberally rewarded, being advanced in five years from plain gentleman to Sir Walter, and made, besides, Warden of the Stannaries, Lieutenant of Cornwall, Vice-Admiral of Devon and Cornwall, and Captain of the Yeomen of the Guard. He was knighted in 1584, the year of the Virginia Charter, and took up at the same time his residence in Durham House, where from his study in a turret overlooking the Thames he commanded a prospect 'as pleasant perhaps as anything in the world.' Profitable patents supplied some part of his profuse expenditure; he had grants of land in Ireland and England; and when all else failed, or more commonly for love, he carried on the West Country trade of privateering, holding, like all West Countrymen, that to rob the King of Spain, who was the Thief of the World, could never be a sin in sea-divinity. Hardly a year passed when his ships did not strike some rich prey, hovering off the Azores in the track of the Portuguese carracks and the galleons of New Spain. His sailors loved him. When the great and rich *Madre de Dios* was brought into Dartmouth in 1592, Ralegh had to be sent for to the Tower, where he was then doing penance, to control his men.

> I assure you, Sir [wrote Robert Cecil], his poor servants, to the number of 140 goodly men, and all the mariners, came to him with shouts of joy; I never saw a man more troubled to quiet them.

His post of Vice-Admiral of Devon and Cornwall took him often to these parts, where, but for his patents, which sometimes vexed the good citizens of Exeter, he was popular and admired. One of his first acts when he became prosperous was to offer to buy the farm-house of Hayes, where he was born, and to the end of his life he spoke with a broad Devon accent which he had no wish to refine.

And yet, in his outward relations—his family, his servants and mariners, and some friends excepted—he was not generally happy. No man in his station had ever more opportunities of popularity than Ralegh, and no man more consistently declined them. In his lowest as in his highest fortunes there is ever this gesture of disdain: 'The World . . . to which I am nothing indebted.' That it was a fault he has himself confessed, but thought the time gone by to mend.

> It is true, that I never travailed after men's opinions, when I might have made the best use of them; and I have now too few days remaining to imitate those that either out of extreme ambition or extreme cowardice, or both, do yet (when death hath them on his shoulders) flatter the world between the bed and the grave.

He was reported 'damnably proud'; and for this, and a

certain insolent splendour that he bore about with him, even more than for his Court favour and his privileges, he was for the greater part of his courtiership hated by the people. He is described by one as 'a tall, handsome, bold man'; by another as having

> a good presence in a handsome and well-compacted person, a strong natural wit and a better judgment, with a bold and plausible tongue, whereby he could set out his parts to the best advantage.

His portraits, which are numerous, mostly exhibit him in middle age, and confirm each other and these impressions. Tall and well-made, sumptuously clothed (as in the portrait from 'the parlour at Downton,' now in the National Portrait Gallery) in a white satin doublet, embroidered with rich pearls, and a great chain of great pearls about his neck, he looks at us coolly and a little scornfully from the canvas, the eyes grey, lips full and firm, hair, beard, and moustache thick and curly (the beard turning up naturally, which gave him an advantage over the gallants of his time), and then, to qualify the challenge of the rest, the forehead astonishingly high and smooth. He was a man throughout his life much gazed at and noted, and had a lofty, telling way of doing things. 'The nature of the man,' says his best biographer, Mr. Stebbing,

> was that he could touch nothing but immediately it appropriated itself to him. He is fabled to have been the first to import mahogany into England from Guiana. He set orange trees in the garden of his wife's uncle, Sir Francis Carew, at Beddington; and he has been credited with their first introduction. The Spaniards first brought potatoes into Europe. Harriot and Lane first discovered them in North Carolina. He grew them at Youghal, and they became his. Harriot discoursed learnedly on the virtues of tobacco, and Drake conveyed the leaf to England. Ralegh smoked, and none but he had the repute of the fashion. . . . For words, ways, and doings he was the observed of all observers. He was active in twenty different ways at once. He was always before the eyes of the world. His name was on every lip.

So versatile a man might have been expected to be superficial. It is a fault not yet discovered in Ralegh. Whatever
he did he worked hard, as a man to whom ease was pleasant
and idleness a curse. All his life he could, if occasion demanded, 'toil terribly.' He was an indefatigable reader,
whether by sea or land, and took always a trunk of books
with him aboard ship. He loved companies where men
talked freely, and whether he was discussing free will with
Marlowe and Harriot, or archaeology with Camden, talking
projects with Dee, or literature with Ben Jonson, he was
equally of the circle and at ease. He is said to have founded
the Mermaid Club. Being a rich student, he made a good
patron. A book of music is dedicated to him as to a virtuoso,
and a book of medicine as to a practitioner. He brought
Spenser and his 'Faerie Queene' to Court. But above all else
he was devoted to inquiries of voyaging and navigation
(Hakluyt and his Voyages owed much to Ralegh), and to
the problems of discovery and the planting of new lands.
He brooded on schemes more daring than Englishmen had
yet attempted: no 'journeys of Picory,' or running 'from
Cape to Cape, and from place to place, for the pillage of
ordinary prizes'; he would mix statecraft with his buccaneer-
ing, and advancing at a bound on the primitive grandeurs
of the Drakes and Hawkins, be the English Cortes or Pizarro.
His dream of an Empire of Guiana, and of 'that great and
golden city which the Spaniards call El Dorado, and the
Naturals Manoa,' persisted, beside the calmer vision of
Virginia, to the end; and in the end, it may be said, he
sacrificed his life to it. Inaction made his dreams sombre.
It was a misfortune which he had often cause to deplore that
the Queen so seldom let him go to sea. In the Armada fight
of '88, though of the Council of War, he had no command,
but served in his own ship as a volunteer. He planned raids
on Spain and on Panama, but always at the last moment
he was forbidden or recalled. It came to be said that he did
not really wish to go—that he was become too easy and
luxurious, and therefore employed others. He never saw
Virginia, nor, probably, would he ever have seen Guiana,

or sailed as Vice-Admiral in the Cadiz and the Islands Expeditions, had he not at these times been an exile from Court.

When Elizabeth died, Ralegh, after twenty-two years in her service, was at the height of his fortunes. He was now fifty-one, and, for a warlike prince, as fit a counsellor, perhaps, as any man in England. James, however, was not warlike; the rest was ordained. The reign had hardly begun when Ralegh was arrested on a charge of conspiracy in the Spanish interest against the Royal person and succession—Ralegh, whose life had been a crusade against Spain, and whose writings had been so many peals and trumpet calls against Spanish tyranny and lust. He was condemned to death, reprieved, and sent to the Tower. The suddenness and injustice of his fall, the circumstances of brutality which attended his trial, and the dignity, manliness, and ability of his defence, made a deep impression on all his friends and on a great many who had been his enemies. This feeling was never lost; it grew with the slow years of his imprisonment, broke into fury over his scaffold and transformed the memory of one of the best hated men in England into that of a martyr and a patriot hero. Of his life in the Tower, where he lived not uncomfortably with his wife and family, of his reading and experiments, and the visits of his friends, much might be written. His mind was never more active. He wrote freely on contemporary affairs; framed text-books of arts and policy for the Prince of Wales, who openly admired him (none but his father, he said, would keep such a bird in a cage); and with that unconquerable courage which had supported him so often, like one that had never had leisure before, sat down, at the age of fifty-five, to write a *History of the World*. His learned friends helped him, but for the most part his mind marched alone. This book, which did not pass its first volume, was his companion for seven years, and contains, in stray sentences and deliberate digressions, his riper experience and philosophy of life. It is grave and melancholy, and in its music winds between the violoncello and the horn, wooing the eloquence of 'just and mighty Death.' It was

published in 1614, in the eleventh year of his captivity;
became one of the formative books of the century; and was
a favourite with such good judges as Cromwell, Hampden,
and Pym. What value Ralegh had for his own writings is
not clear, but it is observable that the only three which he
published in his lifetime—*The Last Fight of the Revenge, The
Discovery of Guiana,* and *The History of the World*—are also his
best. He was a fine poet; but his verses are for the most part
unclaimed, and lie with the common stock of Elizabethan
poetry. Perhaps the sentence of his that lives truest to-day
and comes nearest to our hearts, is this, said after all his
failures, of his colony of Virginia: 'I shall yet live to see it
an English nation.'

'But it is time,' as he would say, 'to beat a retreat.' What
hopes he had of the gold of Guiana, when he left the Tower
on that last desperate adventure, can never be determined,
nor shall we venture to decide of what degree of treachery
King James was guilty when he gave Ralegh's field-state and
itinerary to the Spanish Ambassador. What is certain is that
Ralegh lost his son and his venture, and suffered death himself, and that he was spoken of in Spain as James's sacrifice
to the Spanish Match. That a career so splendid should have
terminated on the scaffold must excite compassion, but
should not in itself surprise the reader of history, which, if
it teaches anything, teaches the philosophy of decline and
fall, and is never so happy or so confident as when describing
the high summer and impending autumn of its theme, and
Destiny the pagan at work upon the gifts of Providence.
Only, when injustice has been done, when the mousing owls
have pulled down the hawk, let us summon the words which
Jerome of Prague made use of at his trial, and which came
to pass: *Post centum annos vos cito.*

THE YOUTH OF MILTON

I

London and Cambridge

ONE of the most interesting developments of literary biography is the growing fashion of studying the youth of great poets. It was not until the nineteenth century that the early years of a poet began to interest the biographer. The boyish verses of Milton, his two versions of the Psalms, so deeply interesting in the history of his mind, are dismissed by Dr. Johnson as compositions which 'in any numerous school'—so he puts it—'would have obtained praise, but not excited wonder.' They are judged merely as prize poems: as competing entries for the trophy of precocity; what they reveal of the young poet's mind and heart is not conceived as a rewarding study. Milton's confessions of early heartaches are passed over as of no account in a biography which is hastening always to the poet of *Paradise Lost*, and to Adam, who, you will remember, had also never been young.

In our day the biography of poets begins, not with the grown man, but with childhood and youth, with those years when the dedication of the poet is made. In that dew and fresh spring of the mind, the natural world, consciously or half-consciously, streams in a million impressions through the delighted senses, with hints of something greater still. Test a man's memories of his childhood, their vividness and tenderness, and you test to that degree his capacity for poetry.

This industrious pursuit of origins and adolescence in biography has, however, its dangers, and of some of these modern dangers I observe that Milton was precociously aware. He speaks of that 'zeal of the next Age,' that heeds more 'the Person than the Doctrine,' or, as we might say, is keener about the author than about his works, about the writer than his message. The place is in his tract of *Prelatical Episcopacy*, and the subject is the early progress of the Gospel.

'Wherever,' he says, 'a man who had bin any way conversant with the Apostles, was to be found, thither flew all the inquisitive ears, although the exercise of right understanding was chang'd into the curiosity of impertinent fabling; where the Mind was to be edify'd with solid Doctrine, there the Fancy was sooth'd with solemn Stories: with less fervency was studied what Saint Paul or Saint John had written, than was listen'd to one that could say—here he taught, here he stood, this was his stature; and thus he went habited, and O happy this house that harbour'd him, and that cold stone whereon he rested, this Village wherein he wrought such a Miracle, and that pavement bedew'd with the warm effusion of his last blood . . . Thus while all their thoughts were pour'd out upon circumstances, and the gazing after such Men as had sat at table with the Apostles . . . by this means they lost their time, and truanted in the fundamental grounds of saving knowledge, as was seen shortly by their Writings.'

I will name no names, but this, I think, comes home. It was to be verified by 'the next Age' upon himself, and even in his lifetime. He became in his last years an object of pilgrimage, and there were foreigners who in his lifetime came expressly to see the house and the chamber in Bread Street where he was born. Aubrey was busy about Milton's stature soon after his death. ('It was not short and thick,' says another researcher, 'but would have been so had he been something shorter and thicker than he was.') His stature, complexion, the colour of his eyes and hair, his dress, his habits—all are anxiously ascertained and noted. The respect for his birthplace was gradually extended indeed to the whole series of his habitations. 'I cannot but remark,' says Johnson, 'a kind of respect, perhaps unconsciously, paid to this great man by his biographers: every house in which he resided is historically mentioned, as if it were an injury to neglect naming any place that he honoured by his presence.' Johnson, who sometimes derided 'the votaries,' as he calls them, the idolaters of Milton, casts no ridicule on this fondness: eight months later he was meekly noting down for Boswell, another votary, a list of his own successive residences in the same city. It is ironical that Johnson should have become more votary-ridden than any other English writer. In many ways he dealt hardly by Milton; but the 'votaries' had sickened him. 'We have had too many honeysuckle lives of Milton,' he told Malone. Mine shall be 'in another strain.' He kept his word; but he also kept to his death the brightest and most romantic of all possible Milton relics: a lock of his auburn hair; acquired by Addison from the poet's daughter, it descended to Johnson, and was possessed thereafter by at least two English poets, Leigh Hunt and Robert Browning. Hunt wrote three poems on receiving it; and showing it to Keats, drew from him a better poem than all the three.

Milton belongs to the great family of Cockney poets. He was born in Bread Street in the City of London on Friday, the 9th of December 1608, at half-past six in the morning. He was not only a Londoner: he was, as his biographer Masson says, a Londoner 'of the innermost circle.' So close indeed does Bow Church stand to what was Milton's father's house, that 'had the famous Bells fallen,' Masson warns us, 'they might have crushed the infant in his cradle.' As we know, the Bells behaved admirably. Masson, a perfervid Scot, exults in these suppositions: they are his reward for that immense antiquarian toil on the life and times of Milton by which we lighter-armed adventurers contrive to profit. But we may sometimes smile. Having to describe the exceptional opportunities open to a spirited and curious lad living in Bread Street—a few steps from all the glory of Cheapside, and the romance of the river—a street, moreover, with the Mermaid Tavern not merely near but actually in it —he breaks out—supposing Shakespeare on his way to a jovial meeting there:

'Nay, if we will imagine the precise amount of personal contact that there was or could have been between Shakespeare and our poet, how else can we do so than by supposing that, in that very year 1614 when the dramatist paid his last visit to

London, he may have spent an evening with his old comrades at the Mermaid, and, going down Bread Street with Ben Jonson on his way, may have passed a fair child of six playing at his father's door, and, looking down at him kindly, have thought of a little grave in Stratford churchyard, and the face of his own dead Hamnet?'

This is not exactly a model for biography: but it is a style by which no one to-day is likely to be betrayed. It is the chief weakness in Masson: the dropping oil of sentiment mingles with the honest sweat of his brow. But there must be something irresistibly appealing in this hypothetical encounter of Shakespeare and the child Milton. Even that great man, Walter Raleigh, succumbs to it: 'perhaps his cloak brushed the child Milton in the street.'

Most of our information about Milton's boyhood and youth came from himself. He is one of the Poets, and they are some of the greatest, most profoundly impressed with the mystery and obligation of their own beginnings. If any defence, indeed, were necessary for studying with some care the youth of Milton, it is to be found in his own works: in the emphasis he always lays, in his autobiographical passages, on his early years. He has told us, or we may discover, in his early poems and letters, and in some places in his more public writings, more than we know of the youth of any first-rate English poet before Pope.

A great part of these revelations is to be found in poems, letters, and college exercises, written in the Latin language, and for that reason not often or very carefully read. Most of the poems had been long before the public when he died, but the *Familiar Letters* we owe most probably to accident: though it is observable that he had kept copies. They were sent to the press in the last year of his life—he had been selling his books and may have been clearing his desk—and, by another accident, to make up a volume, he allowed his old Latin college exercises to go out to the world with the rest. Masson rightly takes credit for being the first biographer of Milton to incorporate all these pieces without exception in the story of his life: but his handling of them is by no means final—his thumb is too broad. Nor was he altogether just to his predecessors. Thomas Warton, in his almost perfect commentary on the Minor Poems of Milton, and after Warton, Todd, display a complete and easy knowledge of everything that Milton wrote, in any language, in prose or verse; not omitting even those college exercises. Johnson asserted emphatically that 'nothing but veneration for Milton's name would now procure those exercises a reader.' Yet there are things to be learned from them, both about Milton and about his poetry.

Nothing is clearer than that Milton was regarded, from his earliest years, as a select child. 'My father destined me,' he says, 'while yet a little child, for the study of humane letters.' It is the passage in the *Defensio Secunda* (1654) beginning with the proud words:

Londini natus Sum:

'I am a Londoner born.' No man was ever prouder of London than Milton: 'the capital city,' as he calls it, 'of the world.' Where else, he asks, can such infinite diversions be found. To be sent down from College (as he was from Cambridge) is a privilege, he says, when one's home is in London. Cambridge indeed!

> *Me tenet urbs reflua quam Thamesis alluit unda*
> *Meque nec invitum patria dulcis habet.*

'I, well content, where Thames with influent tide
My native city laves, meantime reside.'

Who, of free choice, would exchange it for the Cambridge marshes and the reedy Cam, when he might live in London, in glory, by the Thames:

> 'O city, founded by Dardanian hands
> Whose towering front the circling realms commands,
> Too blest abode! no loveliness we see
> In all the earth, but it abounds in thee!

Where will you find such girls as London boasts?—London, with its crowded brilliant streets, its gay and shaded public walks, its theatres (*sinuosi pompa theatri*), its bookstalls ('Meet me,' he writes to a friend, *inter bibliopolas*—among the book-shops).

Is this, then, Charles Lamb, we ask, or John Milton? It is Milton truly, Milton when young, and Milton as he has not been often enough represented. Such is the power of London, to make all its lovers talk alike! As he grew older, he praised it for other things; his pride of citizenship grew with his age:

> 'Behold now this vast City: a City of refuge, a mansion-house of liberty, . . . anvils and hammers waking . . . pens and heads . . . sitting by their studious lamps, musing, searching . . . others as fast reading, trying all things . . .'

With one interval he was to spend nearly all his life in London, and to make, so far as I remember, only one complaint. He complains of the smells and the sewers in a famous Satanic simile in *Paradise Lost*.

The position which Milton gives to his father in the formation of his life is probably not exaggerated. 'I had, from my first years, by the ceaseless care and diligence of my father (whom God recompense) been exercised to the tongues and some sciences . . . both at home and at the schools.' An almost equal service was his early habituation of his son to music. Milton's earliest poems are rich in the sound of all instruments—from the jocund rebeck to the pealing organ—and when he thinks of Heaven, it is of the music of the spheres, the silver trumpets of angels, and the golden harps and choirs of the immortal spirits. When he set up school for those young scamps his nephews, he made choristers of them at once, and he played and sang himself to the last. I have always felt that the foundations of that concerted and solemn harmony in which Milton excels all other English poets were laid in the musical evenings at his father's house in Bread Street.

What his home was like you may learn from his nineteenth century biographer, Masson, who writes, though a Victorian, as if he had been privileged to be present when the family was most alone. 'It was a warm and happy home. . . . During the day the scrivener is busy with his clients, but in the evening the family are gathered together, the father on one side, the mother on the other, the eldest girl Anne and her brother John seated near, and little Kit lying on the hearth.' See what can be done, with a warm imagination, by merely knowing the age of a family!

But he goes further, and brings in the neighbours. There is the Rev. Mr. Stocks, their vicar; Humphrey Lownes, a Bread Street publisher; and John Lane, an acquaintance of Mr. Milton's, and a bad poet.

Masson takes it upon himself to write them all in (and why not Shakespeare, when he was at it, about a lease?), and having seated them, imagines the embarrassment of Lownes lest their well-meaning host should ask him to publish Lane's poetry. It was, as we are always told, a Puritan household: that is to say, Low Church—with a plain bourgeois sense of things in Church and State.

Milton's first tutor seems to have been the Rev. Thomas Young, all the way from Luncarty in Perthshire. The great dogmatic Englishmen seem to attract the Scot: Johnson has his Boswell, and Milton his Masson. Milton had a sincere regard for Young, and the first of his printed letters is written to him, in March 1625, when he was an undergraduate on vacation: 'in London,' he says, 'amid City distractions (*diverticula*), and not, as usual, surrounded with books.' The letter, it is true, is in the main an apology for not having written to his old tutor for three years, and is a repository of ingenious undergraduate excuses: but the epistle in verse which appears to have accompanied it is of a different cast. Milton names Young as the man who first introduced him to the poets, and what is more, sealed him of the order of poets. For so I interpret the line '*Castalio sparsi laeta ter ora mero,*

> First led by him through sweet Aonian shade,
> Each sacred haunt of Pindus I survey'd;
> And favour'd by the muse, whom I implored,
> Thrice on my lip the hallow'd stream I pour'd.'

This 'thrice' is the ritual of enchantment, of the charm: as when Sabrina, by backward magic, releases the spell in *Comus*:

> Thrice upon thy fingers tip
> Thrice upon thy rubied lip. . . .

I name Young more particularly, because we have no record that St. Paul's School, which Milton attended later, did more than its duty by him. It made him a good scholar.

He owed, however, to his attendance there, the principal friendship of his life. Charles Diodati was a few months younger, and of a disposition the best possible for a companion of Milton: serious, but with cheerfulness always breaking through. The early death of this friend must be regarded as one of the severest losses which Milton was to suffer: much bitterness and unhappiness might have been prevented or corrected if Diodati had lived. Diodati went to Oxford, and they corresponded (oddly, as it now seems to us) in Greek and Latin. There are two Greek letters of Diodati's in the British Museum, with, what I am afraid is characteristic, one or two marginal corrections of the Greek in Milton's hand. Or perhaps this was one of the purposes of the correspondence. 'Cheer up!' writes Diodati in 1625. 'It has been bad weather, but it's going to be all right. We'll have our outing after all: for the air and sun and streams and trees and birds and earth and men (he knew all these words) will keep holiday and laugh with us.' (This is the right spirit). He goes on, however:

> *And, be it said without offence, dance with us.*

This is less well, and smells of Puritanism, of the Brownists: but it is only for a moment. 'Be ready to start when I call for you, or come for me.'

The second letter is from Cheshire in the following year, and is an entreaty to Milton to throw his books aside.

'But you, wonder that you are, why do you despise the gifts of nature? Why do you go on hanging night and day over books, and compositions? Live—Laugh—Enjoy your Youth and the hours as they pass—and drop for a time those tiresome researches! You are a martyr to overwork. I am, I admit, in all things else your inferior, but in this I have the better of you, that I have some sense of measure in my labours. Farewell and be merry. . . .'

Milton had all his life too little of this sort of advice, but when Diodati gave it he sometimes took it. He was an unmerciful reader, and when the fit was on him, forgot all else. 'My books,' he says, in a letter of this time to Diodati, 'my books that are my very life.'

Milton spent seven years at Cambridge as a Commoner, from his sixteenth to his twenty-fourth year, and on the whole, if we are to believe him, he did not like it. His College, Christ's, was distinguished enough: Latimer and Leland had been there, and Sir Philip Sidney. Masson would obviously have preferred that he had gone to Trinity as being 'numerically the most important': but is comforted by observing that Christ's stood at least second in numbers of the sixteen Colleges, and in any case, was 'one of the most comfortable colleges in the University.' It is evidently a disappointment to him that Milton had no scholarship or exhibition from St. Paul's, though several were granted in his year: but Milton must often have disappointed the believers in scholastic and professional rewards. He came without a subsidy, and he left without a fellowship. In the list of B.A.s of his year his name stands half-way down: and Masson hastens to point out that the order in such lists was no doubt accidental. In the list of M.A.s of his year his name however stands first, and Masson now believes that the order of names may 'mean something': that the accident of the order may be exaggerated. 'Is the circumstance that his name stands first purely accidental; or are we to suppose that, when the twenty-seven graduates from Christ's appeared before the Registrar, Milton was, by common consent, called on to sign first?' (Dear old Masson! These sentimental suppositions! This tremulous championship of his hero at any moment of his life!)

There was a great public ceremony in the University, and a Latin speech was called for from one of the undergraduates of Christ's. Was Milton chosen? If only Masson could have said he was! He was not: but that young wag, Jack Cleveland, the future Royalist poet, much Milton's junior in the College. Masson at once decides that the practice must have been to choose the youngest member of the College for such duties. In any case, 'Milton,' had the task been assigned to him, 'would,' he assures us, 'have performed it far better.' These are exercises of a very touching solicitude: of which nothing need be said except that Milton didn't want them then, and doesn't need them now.

Milton had his own views of what he was at Cambridge for, and they were not always the views either of his tutors or of his contemporaries. What he principally desired was to be let alone; and this unfortunately is what one's educators cannot readily be brought to do. They are under the impression that in some odd way they are being of assistance to their pupils. I have no doubt that Milton was difficult: the principal feature of his character at this time seems to have been a loathing and hatred of interruption of any sort. He complains, also, more than once in his letters, that he can find 'hardly any real companions' in Cambridge, to share his studies with, and deplores the superficiality of the Cambridge undergraduate. He looks forward to the vacations when he can get by himself, and read. O, what peace and delight that will be, far from these noises.

Milton, both as an undergraduate and in later life, spoke with no great admiration of the University—or indeed of universities—and gave his reasons. A good many poets have passed through Oxford and Cambridge: very few have acknowledged any lasting obligation to either. There is nothing strange in this. Universities proceed, and must proceed, by prescription; and most of the subjects prescribed, the mode of pursuing them, prescription itself, are naturally uncongenial to a young man who is just discovering that his subject is the world. The principal business of the poets during their undergraduate pupillage has been, and always will be, Rebellion.

Sir Walter Raleigh, who knew both places, used to amuse himself with the common statement that Cambridge has *produced* more poets than Oxford. He held it more accurate to say, that many more poets had *resided* at Cambridge than at Oxford. 'Production' was the wrong word: no University *produces* poets. Truer to say that Cambridge had *permitted* more poets among her undergraduates; that she had stifled, maimed, or silenced fewer poets than Oxford. And he believed that the great part of the explanation lay in the different studies of the two places, or rather the different emphasis put upon them. 'The obvious and glaring inhumanity,' he would say, 'of the intellectual exercises most in fashion at Cambridge preserved the poets among her undergraduates from ever supposing that they could care for them: in fact, drove them to poetry. Whereas Oxford, with her seductive humanities, turned her embryo poets into mere dons, or journalists, or Cabinet ministers.'

It is perhaps needlessly well known that Milton got into trouble with his College authorities in his first year: there was a quarrel with his tutor: and he was sent down to remind him of the respect due to authority. He took it very well; didn't lose a term; and was given another tutor whom he seems to have liked. He enjoyed, as we observed, his rustication in London: reading, walking, attending the theatre, and gazing with modest rapture on the girls of London. It was generally in London that these adventures took place.

It has sometimes been said that Milton never wrote of Love like other poets: but whoever said so cannot have read his poems. Two years later, on May Day, 1628, we have the frankest confession that his heart has been touched: and once more by a girl of London. He had scorned Cupid, but Cupid was revenged.

> Hanc memor objecit nobis malus ille Cupido
> Solus et hos nobis texuit ante dolos.
> Nec procul ipse vafer latuit, multaeque sagittae,
> Et facis a tergo grande pependit onus.
> Nec mora; nunc ciliis haesit, nunc virginis ori,
> Insilit hinc labiis, insidet inde genis;
> Et quascunque agilis partes jaculator oberrat,
> Hei mihi! mille locis pectus inerme ferit.

THE YOUTH OF MILTON

> Protinus insoliti subierunt corda furores;
> Uror amans intus, flammaque totus eram.

(Cupid, mindful, malicious, set this maiden in my path; his work alone it was, he wove these wiles. Himself, he lay in hiding hard by. Many an arrow had he, and from his back there hung a great load of torches. Quick in his motions, he settled now on her eyelids, now on her face, then on her lips, then on her cheeks. And whatsoever parts of her he traverses, agile archer, woe betide me, he wounds my undefended heart in a thousand places. Forthwith, frenzies new to me entered my breast. I am in love and on fire within. All that I am was become flame.)

Milton wrote a good deal of verse at Cambridge in a witty academic and local style which places him among the ancestors of the band of university comic poets which includes Gray, and Calverley, and Stephen, and Godley, and Quiller-Couch. It is an odd compartment for Milton to occupy, and he did not occupy it long.

All Milton's verse of this period, both Latin and English, is overshadowed by his great *Ode on the Morning of Christ's Nativity*, the greatest achievement of his Cambridge time, and manifestly the work of a great poet. If it had been lost to us, we might still have recovered some of the sensations of exalted power and mastery which so evidently came upon him at this time, in his Latin elegy of the same date (Christmas 1629, when Milton was twenty-one) written to his friend Diodati.

> At tu si quid agam scitabere (si modo saltem
>   Esse putas tanti noscere siquid agam).
> Paciferum canimus caelesti semine regem,
>   Faustaque sacratis saecula pacta libris;
> Vagitumque Dei, et stabulantem paupere tecto
>   Qui suprema suo cum patre regna colit;
> Stelliparumque polum, modulantesque aethere turmas,
>   Et subito elisos ad sua fana Deos.
> Dona quidem dedimus Christi natalibus illa;
>   Illa sub auroram lux mihi prima tulit.
> Te quoque pressa manent patriis meditata cicutis;
>   Tu mihi, cui recitem, judicis instar eris.

It is plain that early in his life Milton came to the decision that poetry is a profession and that poets are, in the general guild and corporation of letters, a special, and, as it were, a vowed order of men. Of this vow—taken privately as between themselves and those powers of the mind of which they are conscious, and watched over by the source of all true inspiration, which is the Divine—of this vow, so taken and so guarded, there are two principal injunctions: (1) against haste and unripeness and extemporary vanity: an injunction of study; (2) of virtue; or, as Milton, like Plato, felt it—musically—against discord of the soul. The poet must be himself a good man if he is to be a good poet; for true poetry is no other than the music of the soul. The harmony of virtue and the discord of vice Milton clearly felt from very early years; with that turn which he had even then, and had always, more than any other of our poets, for figuring the Creation, and all the operations of its members as a universal hymn or symphony to the Creator and the Spirit of Good. The Poet, above all men, must, he passionately felt, be in tune with this harmony, and must be pure even to *hear* it, which is the first and last privilege of poets, and the ground of that reverence which in all decent and thoughtful communities is paid to poets by ordinary men. Nowadays, we are inclined to say that a poet *sees* things that ordinary men do not see. Wordsworth saw things, we say, which were there because he saw them. Milton, like the ancients, habitually thinks of a poet as *hearing* things that ordinary men cannot hear, and that long before his blindness—indeed all his life. He was not unfamiliar with the rewards and ecstasies of Vision. After the harmony of sound there is nothing so nobly praised or so luxuriously enjoyed by Milton as the element of Light. But habitually he listens, and his inspiration comes to him by ear in the early calm of mornings. Milton's blindness, for this reason, crippled him less than might have been supposed for his essential task. His planetary harmonies came to him clearer and more fully toned. There is in all men, and especially in poets and artists, a constant competition of the senses, which are greedy things, craving to be fed. We may think of Milton's blindness, not cruelly or unfeelingly, as a reduction of this competition, and a concentration of power.

2

Horton, and the 'Laureat Fraternity of Poets'

Milton left Cambridge in his twenty-fourth year, and after some argument with his family about an alternative profession, having definitely decided against entering the Church, persuaded them to trust him. Two documents survive from this family discussion: a letter to an elderly friend who had expostulated, and at a later stage, when the discussion had been revived, a verse epistle to his father. The result was never in doubt. Milton was correct, but firm. He had a will of iron, and he had his way. Do not think, he tells the friend, that I am insensible to ambition. I am not. Or to the conveniences and natural expectations of life: an establishment some day, and children of my own. Or that I am wholly sunk in dreams, like Endymion with the Moon. I know what my task is to be, and it is one for which I am not ready, nor can be ready. Give me time. I plan even now, 'with a sacred reverence and religious advisement, how best to *undergo*, not taking thought of being *late*, so it give advantage to be more *fit*.' He seals the bond with that Petrarchan stanza on his three-and-twentieth year, which ends so gravely, and with so little of the brag of youth:

> Yet, be it less or more, or soon or slow,
> It shall be still in strictest measure even
> To that same lot, however mean or high,
> Towards which Time leads me, and the will of Heaven.
> All is, if I have grace to use it so,
> As ever in my great Task-Master's eye.

The same self-will, resolution, and consciousness of a higher destination, appears in the youth of Wordsworth: the same charges of aimlessness, the same anxiety of friends, the same profound disinclination for the drudgery of a profession: the belief, as Milton puts it, that 'God delights not to make a drudge of virtue, whose actions must be all elective and unconstrained.' Milton has indeed already found a profession, but a profession, as his father must have ruefully considered, in which no money was to be made, a profession without visible establishment, of which the rewards, as a rule, are lavishly post-dated, and payable by posterity.

The life of the poet and man of letters is nowadays well enough understood; our poets have taught us that their indolence is not all idle. But Milton's father had less to guide him; and though he consented at first, as the years passed, he grew uneasy once more. It was then, I suppose, when his son's retirement had lasted some years, that the Latin epistle was written, *Ad Patrem*. It is a charming poem, from any son to any father: an affectionate appeal *ad hominem* (Come, father, he seems to say, you a Musician, run down poetry! The Arts, in this Philistine world, should stand by each other!). He acknowledges his obligations to his father: they can never be repaid, and he has nothing to pay with: only gratitude and poetry. But what a heavenly coinage this poetry is! His father, if any one, should know, having set so much of it to music. Why should he be surprised that a son of his turns out a poet—musician father, poetical son—what more natural, or more becoming! Phoebus Apollo, arithmetically inspired, has gifted half of himself to me, and the other half to my parent, Music and Song, 'so that, father and son, we have the whole god between us!' A matter, surely, for family congratulation!

Come—you are only pretending. You are a merchant, it is true, but you are not like other merchants. You do not rate everything by the money it brings in. You wouldn't really, would you, send me on the Exchange, or doom me to the noise and clatter of the Law-courts? Rather, surely, to the retirement of the mind, far from the city's hum, where at my will I may walk all day with Apollo by my side.

Consider: there is nothing you have not done to equip me for the life of letters: and it is the life of letters I would choose. To an expensive classical education I have added, on your advice, a knowledge of French, Italian, even Hebrew, and the natural sciences of the earth and the heavens. The time is come when I must gaze on knowledge brow to brow, all cloud removed. See, she bends her face, naked now and fully-seen, to the print of my kisses! Can I refuse? You would not allow me, surely, if I could.

These, father, he ends, are youthful verses; but if my writings shall live, this tribute of praise may preserve to ages unborn my parent's name!

Is this last a bribe? It is a reminder, at any rate, of the poet's *quid pro quo*. But Mr. Milton the scrivener needed no such bribe. He was won already, and stands high to this day among the good fathers of history.

Milton spent nearly six years in retirement at Horton—from his twenty-fourth to his thirtieth year—among the water-meadows of Buckinghamshire: reading, meditating, composing, and luxuriating (as his poems show) in country pleasures. He was never to be again so near to the heart and the common life of England. Sometimes, he tells us, he would ride into London, to buy books, or take a lesson in Music and the Mathematics. But for the most part he lived quietly in Horton, indulging, as it has been said of Hazlitt, 'the only educational experiment worth trying—self-education.' Hazlitt is another of the aimless ones, so rare in the seventeenth century, and so common in the nineteenth, who *made* himself while apparently doing nothing: sitting at home from nineteen to twenty-four, reading, marking, and digesting.

Of course, the money must come from somewhere: scrivening, or the funds. Milton is one of the financed poets of our literature. Till he was over thirty-two he never earned a penny, nor was asked to. We should not have had him otherwise: he is of the class of studious poets, the poets of long views, the meditative, the scholarly, the *docti poetae*, whom the world, from time to time, out of its business earnings, is requested to afford. As I run over their names, from Virgil to Tennyson, I find myself pausing with regret at the great name of Dryden: a poet so manifestly of the same race and lineage, but unfortunately placed: a great poet without money or leisure, and without a patron. He could not afford to prepare himself; to be 'elective and unconstrained'; and so he stands, one of the Titans of English poetry—toiling in chains.

Milton's temperament and habits at this time are not to be inferred from his later controversial pronouncements, and from the passionless routine, so minutely recorded by his biographers, of his later life. Up at four and bed at nine—with every hour its allotted task or recreation—this is the day of an elderly student, with the first sweetness and ravishment of study long past. Milton at Horton lived and studied very differently: working in great bouts, and for weeks at a time wholly carried away and abstracted from the world. 'You must excuse my not writing often,' he says to his friend Diodati. 'You are different. When you are studying you can stop and take breath in the middle; visit your friends—write letters—take a journey. I cannot. My temperament is such that when I am once entered into a subject, no delay, no rest, no care or thought of almost anything can withhold me until I reach the allotted goal, and round off, as it were, some great period of my studies.'

It is important to disengage this vivid portrait of the younger Milton from the more familiar armchair descriptions of his ordered old age. Milton at Horton is almost ideally the young poet of romance: beautiful, intense, distracted, amorous, in love with beauty for itself, and admiring, yet afraid of it in women—delighting, now in solitude, and now in society—a worshipper of pomp and mask and pageant, whether in Nature or in Art—and taking his poetry, without remorse or afterthought—not wistfully, as in his later years—from the exploded superstitions of all ages, from Paganism and Christianity, with sometimes very strange results—from Feudalism, which he was to denounce, and even from popery itself, which he had been trained to abhor. The pleasures of *L'Allegro* are the pleasures of Merry England: Laud and Star Chambers quite forgot; and Evening, in *Comus*, comes on, grayhooded, in the palmer's weed of Rome. 'But poetry,' as Warton says, 'is of all religions; and popery is a very poetical one.' Poetry at all times, with Milton, tended to carry it over doctrine: and he never parted with Romance; but it is whole-hearted only here. It is not fanciful, I think, to attribute some of the heightened grace and gaiety of his earlier poems of this period to his association with the noble family of the Egertons and their friends. He was in no danger of having his head turned by polite society. He had the same corrective at hand as Tennyson in like circumstances: he studied the stars. Tennyson, as enthusiastic an astronomer as Milton, after looking at the clusters in Hercules and Perseus, made this profound remark: 'I cannot think much of the county families after that.'

We are singularly well-informed about this period of Milton's life. He has left us an eloquent account of his studies;[1] and, what is more, we possess the very manuscript book in which he entered his poems. His first and favourite authors, he informs us, had been the smooth elegiac poets of Rome: and even if he had not informed us, we could tell it well enough. The false wit of almost all the Cambridge poems—even of the splendid Nativity Hymn itself—is a treacherous gift from Ovid. One of the most important of the lessons he taught himself at Horton was that Ovid—the style of Ovid—must be outgrown. There are whole stanzas of the Nativity Hymn only saved from ruin by their miraculous prosody. Their meaning will not bear examination; they silence criticism by their sound.

Milton was remarkable, even in his earliest compositions, for his love of divine objects: for the gusto with which he describes things supra-terrestrial. He was remarkable, also, even then, for the extreme materiality of these descriptions, for a style of material ornament of which our Hymn books give a debased and popular version. His Heaven from the first has a local, and almost tangible quality: it had always been a jewelled Heaven, and the wings of his angels had always sparkled with gold and precious stones. For this conception he was indebted not only to his Biblical authority (Ezekiel and the Book of Revelations), but to his classical reading. The richly jewelled descriptions of the Roman poets have

[1] *An Apology for Smectymnuus.*

some share of the responsibility. The angels of Milton were dressed from the same wardrobe as Ovid's Cupid. It was the same brilliant costumier who recommended to him that forecast of the future life, so unintelligible without this background, and so little satisfying to our modern tastes:

'Attir'd with stars we shall for ever sit.'

This jewellery of the Latin elegiac poets spreads itself, in Milton's early work, over the face of nature. Even the beds of his rivers are rough with gems. We see the eighteenth century coming: Nature wears a livery. A thousand liveried angels, we are told in *Comus* 'lackey' Chastity. As he grew older, he economized in these ideas and ornaments, but *Paradise Lost* is still, to our thinking, too heavily encrusted. Part of his poetical history at Horton is, as I said, his gradual desertion of them. He found a better model than Ovid in our own Spenser, whom he devoutly studied; in the great Italian poets, Dante, Petrarch, and their followers (he had already begun to read and to imitate the Italian poets before he left Cambridge); in the dramas of our own Elizabethans (he read the Folio of Shakespeare in its first edition); and in the great dramatists of Greece.

It is observable that in his account of these years Milton passes with particular weight and solemnity to his studies in Greek, and specially to his studies in Greek philosophy.

'Thus, from the laureat fraternity of poets, riper years and the ceaseless round of study and reading led me to the shady spaces of philosophy, but chiefly to the divine volumes of Plato and his equal Xenophon. Where if I should tell ye what I learned of Chastity and Love—I mean that which is truly so, whose charming cup is only virtue, which she bears in her hand to those who are worthy: the rest are cheated with a thick intoxicating potion which a certain sorceress, the abuser of Love's name, carries about—and how the first and chiefest office of love begins and ends in the soul . . . it might be worth your listening.'[1]

He is answering a charge of incontinence, of lewd living,

[1] *An Apology for Smectymnuus* (1692).

so strangely brought against him by his adversaries; and he answers it in the language of his own *Comus*, which is, let me remind you, the language of Plato.

The question has sometimes been raised, of Milton as of Ben Jonson, how much Greek he really knew. It is certain that he knew Latin, as a language, much better. Even as an undergraduate he has the Latin poets at his fingers'-ends, and composes in Latin like a master. In Greek it was not so. There was no public for Greek compositions: and no encouragement to write them. For ten years after leaving school he wrote no Greek: and then one morning, at his favourite time, *sub lucis exortum* (just before dawn)—the time when, all his life, things came to him—he started, on some impulse, to translate a psalm he had paraphrased as a boy, into Homeric hexameters. 'I warn you,' he writes from Horton, 'that this is my first and only Greek composition since I left St. Paul's. My taste, as you know, has been rather for Latin and English composition: and indeed, whoever spends his time in these days on Greek composing, might almost as well be singing to the deaf.' The Homeric hexameters in question have every mark of their impulsive origin, and of an unpractised hand. Johnson has nothing to say about his Greek, and for a good reason. How he would have enjoyed it if he could! Even Landor, who devotes pages to an enthusiastic criticism of Milton's Latin verse, has nothing to say for his Greek. 'We will pass over his Greek verses,' he says. 'They are such as no boy of the Sixth Form would venture to show up in any of our public schools.' One error or misprint has persisted in them from 1645, when they first appeared, to the present day: ἐκτυπέοντα in the 19th line. There is no such word: but ἐκκτυπέοντα will more than pass. Milton wrote two other Greek pieces—both short—and took the trouble to rewrite a line of one of them for the second edition of his *Occasional Poems* in 1673. But he left ἐκτυπέοντα uncorrected. You will permit me the shamelessness of announcing my one Miltonic emendation: now safely incorporated in Professor Grierson's edition. It is a minute but just discernible return for many years of pupillage to the Greek tongue.

Milton had little to learn about Latin poetry when he went to Horton; but about Greek, probably a good deal. I see the first clear signs of his ripened Greek reading in *Comus*. Even its Platonism seems fresher from the source, though he had called himself a Platonist at Cambridge. It is more like Plato and less like Boethius. The ring of the *Dialogues* comes through it, and that teaching of the *Phaedo* about body and spirit which was to colour his theology for life. There is an attempt, even, at the Greek dramatic style; for *Comus* is a garden of experiments. Now it is Shakespeare who is imitated; now Fletcher or Ben Jonson; and now Euripides. There is only one failure, and you will remark that it is in the Greek style. Traces of it are scattered through the first few hundred lines. *Comus*, stopping the dance:

> 'Break off, break off, *I feel the different pace*
> Of some chaste footing near about this ground.'

'Feel the different pace' is from Greek tragedy.

The lost Lady, unwilling to approach the revellers, expresses herself in the same unfamiliar idiom:

> 'Yet O where else
> Shall I inform my unacquainted feet . . .?'

This is not English; and every classical reader knows why and where it comes from.

Still in this style, describing the time and occasion of her brothers' departure:

> 'But where they are, and why they came not back,
> Is now the labour of my thoughts, 'tis likeliest
> They had engag'd their wand'ring steps too far.'

This laborious naïveté about the why and wherefore is one of the strange banalities (or so it seems to us) of the drama of Greece.

Still experimenting, Milton tries what can be done in that line-for-line dialogue, which the Greeks so loved and called stichomythia, and which undergraduates know as cat-and-mouse. It is the central passage of the experiment, and it was decisive. Comus and the Lady meet, and address each other in these lines:

COMUS. What chance, good Lady, hath bereft you thus?
LADY. Dim darkness, and this leafy labyrinth.
COMUS. Could that divide you from near-ushering guides?
LADY. They left me weary on a grassy turf.
COMUS. By falsehood, or discourtesy, or why?
LADY. To seek i' the valley some cool friendly spring.
COMUS. And left your fair side all unguarded, Lady?
LADY. They were but twain, and purpos'd quick return.
COMUS. Perhaps forestalling night prevented them.
LADY. How easy my misfortune is to hit!
COMUS. Imports their loss, beside the present need?
LADY. No less than if I should my brothers lose.
COMUS. Were they of manly prime, or youthful bloom?
LADY. As smooth as *Hebe's* their unrazor'd lips.

Thus far the experiment goes, and surely it had gone far enough. So Milton thought, and abruptly changing the key, plunged his Comus out of Greece into England. This alien and unhappy style is deserted for the native manner of our own dramatists:

Two such I saw, what time the labour'd ox
In his loose traces from the furrow came,
And the swink'd hedger at his supper sat;
I saw them under a green mantling vine,
That crawls along the side of yon small hill,
Plucking ripe clusters from the tender shoots;
Their port was more than human, as they stood;
I took it for a faery vision
Of some gay creature of the element,
That in the colours of the rainbow live,
And play i' the plighted clouds! I was awestruck,
And as I past, I worshipt; if those you seek,
It were a journey like the path to Heaven,
To help you find them.

We are in England again with Shakespeare and *The Tempest.*

One other trace I find in *Comus*—and only one—of Milton's Greek misfortune. It is in the next ten lines:

> To find out that, good Shepherd, I suppose,
> In such a scant allowance of starlight,
> Would overtask the best land-pilot's art,
> Without the sure guess of well-practis'd feet.

Milton, with these words, said good-bye to this style for ever. Not even in *Samson Agonistes* was he more than for a moment tempted to it. It is a style not cut for our climate.

It is possible that some readers are unacquainted with A. E. Housman's composition in this manner. I will quote from it, not merely for its humour, which is excellent, but because, in its good-natured banter, in its mellow ridicule of some of the alien simplicities of Greek tragic dialogue, it confirms Milton's judgment and our own.

> O suitably-attired-in-leather-boots
> Head of a traveller, wherefore, seeking whom,
> Whence, by what way, how purposed art thou come
> To this well-nightingaled vicinity?
> My object in inquiring is to know.
> But if you happen to be deaf and dumb
> And do not understand a word I say,
> Pray wave your hand, to signify as much.

.   .   .   .   .   .

> 1. I journeyed hither a Boeotian road.
> 2. Flying on horseback, or with feet for oars?
> 1. Plying with speed my partnership of legs.
> 2. Beneath a shining or a rainy Zeus?
> 1. Mud's sister, not himself, adorns my shoes.
> 2. May I then learn at what your presence shoots?
> 1. A shepherd's questioned mouth informed me that—
> 2. What? For I know not yet what you will say,—
> 1. Nor will you, ever, if you interrupt—
>   —This house was Agamemnon's, no one's else.
> 2. Nor did he shame his throat with hateful lies.
> 1. May I then enter, passing through the door?

2. Go, chase into the house a lucky foot.
   And, oh my son, be on the one hand good,
   And do not, on the other hand, be bad.
   For that is very much the safer plan.

There are other and more genial signs in *Comus* of the
influence of Greek Tragedy on Milton. He was deep in his
favourite Euripides, and here and there, as will happen,
Euripides peeps out. That very passage I quoted, for its
radiantly Shakespearian and Elizabethan quality: 'Two
such I saw,' etc., has its roots in the *Iphigenia in Tauris* as well
as in *The Tempest*. A young shepherd in that play has a vision
of two bright figures sitting together:

> ἐνταῦθα δισσοὺς εἶδε τις νεανίας
> βουφορβὸς ἡμῶν

> And there two forms a village lad did see
> One of our shepherds . . .

He creeps back ἄκροισι δακτύλοισι—on his finger-tips—or,
as we say, on hands and knees—to report the wonder. 'He
was awe-struck.' 'And as he gazed, he worshipt.' The gravest
of the elder shepherds hails the two beings, supposing them
gods:

> Is it to Lord Palaemon that I speak
> The son of Leukothea of the Sea?

They are, in fact, Orestes, and the brother of Iphigenia,
seeking his sister (it was the similarity of situation which put
Milton in mind of him)—Orestes and his friend Pylades; and
for the moment Milton has no further use for them. But see
the economical workman: see why poets are rightly called
the sons of memory. The shepherd's question was not forgotten. If you will turn 600 lines on, in *Comus* (873), to the
incantation for Sabrina—that learned and lovely roll-call of
the deities of the water—you will find a recollection there:

> By scaly *Triton's* winding shell
> And old sooth-saying *Glaucus'* spell
> By Leucothea's lovely hands
> And her Son that rules the strands. . . .

Here is the Palaemon of the shepherd's question, with his mother of the sea—Leucothea the White Goddess—and observe how he has imagined her—how a great poet conceives his reading. She is the White Goddess, and he is sure (though no one has told him) that she has lovely hands. Why *hands*? It is not a fair question to ask any poet. Why *kisses four*?, says Keats. You may well ask. Because it had to be *four* or *score*, for the rhyme, he says, and a score was too many: 'we must temper the Imagination, as the critics say, with Judgment.' So Keats, in his good humour, to a layman. But if you would really like to know, in this same vein, why it was her *hands* that were lovely, read the next line:

> ' By Thetis' tinsel-slipper'd feet.'

Thetis could not be left out of such a list, and Thetis had always been silver-footed, as Achilles had always been swift. Leucothea's feet (God forbid we should doubt it!), we must assume to have been as lovely as her hands, but *feet* were forestalled.

Milton, in all his reading, fastidiously selects, and all that he selects he reimagines. He could do it as soon almost as he began to write. In his first poem, the Psalm which he translated as a boy of fifteen, Pharaoh is not left there: he is 'the tawny king.' One remembers that. The most hackneyed of the Latins as well as the choicer and less familiar Greeks yield up their life to him: Ovid, even, inkstained by centuries of grimy and reluctant schoolboys. There was a fancy of the ancient world, still surviving in an English phrase, that for seven days of the year, while the Halcyon bird was brooding, the winds fell, and a calm descended on the sea. It was a set topic, and Ovid, who has all the set topics, has this one also:

> Perque dies placidos. . .
> Incubat Halcyone pendentibus aequore nidis.
>
> > (*Metam.* xi, 745-46.)

As one may render it:

> Through the calm days . . .
> The Halcyon broods on pendulous nests at sea.

It is a pretty notion, prettily imaged: and when it was first adventured, it was as fresh as dew. But there is nothing among the Ancients more customary.

Consider now what the undergraduate Milton does with it, in his *Nativity Hymn*:

> The winds with wonder whist,
> Smoothly the waters kist,
> Whispering new joys to the mild ocean,
> Who now hath quite forgot to rave
> While birds of calm sit brooding on the charmed wave.

One would not have thought that ancient bird had so much blood in her. Here is a faded pagan fancy literally new-born, and not only new-born, but *baptized*: enrolled in the universal pageant which proclaims the Birth of Christ.

A short word for this kind of thing is Renaissance. Dead or half-dead reading comes alive. Frayed or hackneyed images are restamped. Whenever and wherever this occurs—in the twelfth, the fourteenth, the sixteenth, the twentieth century —*there* is Renaissance. What we call more specifically *the* Renaissance was merely a moment of time in which this species of miracle occurred oftener and more noticeably than usual. There has always been dead reading. There have always been hackneyed images. There were plenty of both in the time we call the Renaissance. But in that happy time the minority who *hear* and *see, even when they are reading*, was beyond the average of human record. Milton was its last great English representative until the new Romantics, and *Hyperion*.

I have given some examples of this fortunate process, but I have not said how it is done. Of course I cannot tell you, nor can anyone else except by doing it. One thing I *can* tell you. It is not a *hurried* process: nor is it given to the witty and worldly to succeed in it. The ruins and fragments of the ancient world come into no such life and bright outline at the call of the brisk and the clever. I am reminded of the advice of the old Chinese painter, Sung Ti, who was painting when William the Norman conquered England:

> 'You should choose,' he said, 'an old tumbledown wall and throw over it a piece of white silk. Then morning and evening

you should gaze at it, until at length you can see the ruin through the silk—its prominences, its levels, its zigzags, its cleavages, storing them up in the mind and fixing them in the eye. Make the prominences your mountains, the lower parts your water, the hollows your ravines, the cracks your streams. . . . Get all these thoroughly into you, and soon you will see men, birds, plants, and trees, flying and moving among them. You may then ply your brush according to your fancy, and the result will be of heaven, not of men.'

Mysterious! So it is: but so is all creation. Milton and the men of the Renaissance found antiquity Romantic, and even in the artificial tales of Ovid, the delight of a sophisticated court, saw the men and birds and nymphs and trees flying and pursuing and dancing out the great adventure among the immortal ruins of a fallen world. The shrouded but imperishable world of the Ancients is reborn. The piece of white silk, which for the painter is real, for the poet is the ignoring of time and distance. It is the film over the eyes of Keats as he gazes timelessly at the arrested figures on a Grecian Urn.

I have mentioned the manuscript book, in which Milton was accustomed to enter and revise his compositions. The Book itself may be inspected in Trinity College Library, Cambridge, in its handsome red binding of the year 1736. The MS. was found there, derelict and uncatalogued among a lot of loose papers. Birch, the editor of Milton's Prose, drove down to Cambridge the moment he heard of it; transcribed its most important readings, and large parts of it *seriatim*, within a year of its discovery; and published the whole in his Preface to the prose works in 1738. Peck, the antiquary, was close on his heels, and Bishop Newton, Milton's mid-eighteenth century editor, after him.

To see the Book itself is to understand rather better what Charles Lamb felt when he was shown it at Trinity. He wished he had never seen it, and his regret is so poignant that even the editor of the facsimile feels bound to quote him, as if to deprecate in advance such emotions in his own readers.

'I had thought,' says Lamb, 'I had thought of the Lycidas

as a full-grown beauty—as springing up with all its parts absolute—till, in an evil hour, I was shown the original copy of it, together with the other minor poems of the author, in the library of Trinity, kept like some treasure to be proud of. I wish they had thrown them in the Cam, or sent them after the latter cantos of Spenser, into the Irish Channel. How it staggered me to see the fine things in their ore! interlined, corrected! as if their words were mortal, alterable, displace-able at pleasure! as if they might have been otherwise and just as good! as if inspiration were made up of parts, and these fluctuating, successive, indifferent! I will never go into the workshop of any great artist again!'

So Lamb wrote, on impulse, in a footnote to his essay on 'Oxford (which was really Cambridge) in Vacation'; the footnote was not reprinted when he collected the Eliana, and for that reason is not very often read. Can it be that he had changed his mind when he suppressed it? Most scholars and poets, on reflection, will be of the same mind as Birch: that it is extremely agreeable to see the first thoughts and sub-sequent corrections of so great a poet as Milton, and that Mr. Waller's observation was a just one:

> Poets lose half the praise they should have got,
> Could it be known what they discreetly blot.

Milton himself had no delusions about a great artist's work-shop. He knew that nothing perfect comes without labour and correction. The nineteenth century was a little crazed by its workshop of genius and inspiration: and allowed too little for the realities of the craft. Its most monstrous extra-vagance was that pleasant fiction of the mediaeval revival of the last century, that the Gothic cathedrals rose like the visions of a dream under the rhythmical trowels and hammers of singing masons! I am afraid a builder's yard is, and always will be, extremely unlike Paradise. Milton speaks himself, with a full sense of its meaning, of what he calls 'the very critical Art of Composition,' and there is a passage very much to the point in his Tract against Church Government: 'In things artificial,' he says, 'seldom any elegance is wrought without a superfluous waste and refuse in the transaction. No marble statue can be politely carved, no fair edifice built without almost as much rubbish and sweeping.'

Look, then, at the facsimile of his MS. without compunction: and marvel not so much at the interlinings as at the economy and tidiness of his workmanship, and his unerring improvement in revision. I doubt if a single alteration can be found which is not demonstrably an improvement, in sense, or in melody, or in both. One poem, *At a Solemn Music*, we are privileged to see him compose before our eyes, with an *apparatus criticus* which shows these stages. I hope that in the next few years, in the reviving interest that is visible to-day in Milton's text, this deficiency will be supplied.

3

Joannes Miltonius Anglus

The life of a poet, says Milton, should be itself a true poem; and a true poem, says Aristotle, should have a beginning, a middle, and an end. The lives of most of us, I fear, are like those bad poems which have no middle; we are still bustling and beginning when the end comes and huddles up our drama. Milton was not to be so surprised. There are weaknesses of temper in his life, but no weakness in its plan. It has its beginning, its middle, and its end, like the great work of art it was. Only two things, so far as we know, he planned and did not finish: his History of England and his Latin Dictionary.

Milton at school, at college, and in his six years' retirement at Horton, had done everything that seemed to be needed, for his poetic education, except travel; and in the spring of 1638—being then thirty years old—he set out for Italy. Fifteen months later he returned to England, knowing well, as he did so, that the first great period of his life was over. He established himself in London, which was to be his home for the rest of his life, and bent himself to the middle years.

There were signs that he had outgrown his country seclusion—his *rus suburbanum*, as he calls it—some time before he left; his last year at Horton was restless. A desire for human kind was troubling him; for company, and diversions; he talked of taking rooms in the Temple, actually, where he could *see* people. It was time to leave the nest. Three years earlier, when he was writing *Comus* in 1634, he was still happy there, pluming his feathers:

> Wisdom's self
> Oft seekes to sweet retired Solitude
> Where, with her best nurse Contemplation,
> She plumes her feathers, and lets grow her wings
> That in the various bustle of resort
> Were all to-ruffled.

Resort and bustle were precisely what he now longed for; and when that joy had subsided, the other and long-looked-for joy of assured and elaborate poetical performance. 'You ask me,' he wrote to Diodati in September 1637, 'you ask me what I am doing and thinking of. Listen, my friend, and let it be in your private ear, lest I blush. Thinking? Of Immortality, God help me! Doing? Growing my wings and meditating flight.'

Two months later he finished and dated *Lycidas*, November 1637, and these words to Diodati, on that account, assume unusual value. They are the best commentary we shall ever have on that poem and its supposed intrusive egotisms: for they are hotly contemporary, and straight from the heart. Two of the most critical passages in *Lycidas* are musical rewordings of that confession to his friend: the great argument on Fame and Immortality, and the splendid cryptic close.

> Thus sang the uncouth Swain to th' Okes and rills,
> While the still morn went out with Sandals gray,
> He touch'd the tender stops of various Quills,
> With eager thought warbling his *Dorick lay*:
> And now the Sun had stretch'd out all the hills,
> And now was dropt into the Western bay;
> At last he rose, and twitch'd his Mantle blew:
> To-morrow to fresh Woods, and Pastures new.

These grave and splendid lines have sometimes been interpreted as a *political* prophecy, as a prophecy of his part in the approaching troubles of the Civil War and Commonwealth; but I believe it is certain that they have no such intention. We are still in *Lycidas*, nearly four years distant from his first prose pamphlet. It is of Art, not of Politics, that he is thinking: of the Art of Poetry, to which he had dedicated his life. He is announcing, to himself and to all who had ears and would listen, that his Horton period was over; that his novitiate and his seclusion were at an end. The sun that goes down in *Lycidas* goes down in the first full stage of his career. Between the meditation of flight, of which he spoke to Diodati, and the twitcht mantle in the poem, the difference is one of figure and metaphor only. It had come to him, as in the Scriptures it comes to the destined, to the favoured of God, that his time was upon him: 'and he arose and went into another country.'

It had been a long apprenticeship; and it was a somewhat aged apprentice who now crossed to Italy in April 1638, and rounded off his studies with a Grand Tour. But Milton was always a little late: he went late to Cambridge, he went abroad late, he published late: and would have published later if he had been allowed. He was not afraid of lateness, as he has told us: better late than unfit. His business was heroic poetry, and heroic poetry, says a sixteenth century critic, 'is liker a long voyage than anything else: once launched on that wide ocean you cannot trust to petty landfalls, to ports of call, and lighthouse men: you must lay in your supplies before you sail.' Milton knew this Jerome Vida of Cremona, the sixteenth century Italian Bishop—Pope's 'Immortal Vida'—and had praised his verses in the *Nativity Ode*. There can be little doubt that he knew Vida's *Art of Poetry* also: that famous sixteenth century treatise in which the education of the epic poet is sketched from birth. It is remarkable how closely the education of Milton for heroic poetry conforms to the Renaissance ideal. Poetry to Vida, as to Milton, is a sacred calling, for which the novice, once selected, must be segregated; and the selection and segregation cannot come too soon. Vida, like Quintilian with his infant orator, begins at the cradle; engages the child's nurse, and lectures the parents on his tutors. Milton's family, in their treatment of him, came creditably near to Vida's recipe. As the young poet grows to manhood—remote from cities— among pleasing solitudes—lighter pieces, says Vida, will engage his art—elegies and pastorals, his *Eclogues* and his *Georgics* before he tries *Aeneids*. This time-honoured sequence was observed both by Spenser and by Milton, largely because it is true to nature. In the frontispiece of the first edition of Milton's Poems—the book of 1645—the portrait of Milton which is there presented, and which annoyed him so much— it makes him so plain, and he was in reality so handsome— and then Salmasius, his opponent, had the impudence to congratulate him on the excellent likeness—this portrait in the frontispiece is shown against a curtain which has been partially withdrawn, and through the window thus disclosed we see a pastoral clearing by a forest side, and shepherds with their crooks and wallets, and Corydon piping under a tree. The tree is tufted like the groves of the forest in *Comus*, and the timber in the background is of his favourite English elm. It is a partly traditional picture of the *juvenilia* of a heroic poet—for so Milton regarded his *Comus* and *Lycidas*, his *L'Allegro* and *Il Penseroso*—of what is soon to be his youthful past—the pastorals and elegies of the English Virgil—the flights about the nest before the long sea-transit of the epic migration.

The great danger at this pre-epic stage, says Vida, is that the young poet may fall in love. It was a risk which Milton had had to fight more than once, and if a certain dark beauty called, as we now know, Emilia, had taken those Italian sonnets of his quite seriously, it might have ruined half his plans. I call it dangerous, says Vida, because nothing so quickly spoils young poets' work; their verses, somehow, grow *silly*. Afterwards, that is their affair: poets are notoriously susceptible: but at the novice stage, pray, pray avert it.

Rural solitude and study—the Horton period, as we may call it, of Vida's scheme—should be followed, he tells us, as

Milton was now to follow it, by Travel. Milton, therefore, when he set out for Italy, was still following the epic curriculum. The future Virgil, like the Greek Odysseus, must see men and cities, and affairs, and consort with his kind. Feasted and full of this new knowledge, sitting once more, his travels over, with his books around him, he must bend himself, says Vida, to the great decision of his career. The *subject* of the future epic—of the *opus magnum* for which all his life hitherto has been merely schooling—this subject must now be chosen. The choice, of course, will not be made at once. An epic is not like other poems. It is a good deal longer, for one thing. Choosing a subject for an elegy or a pastoral is rather like choosing a mistress: on and off, and no hearts broken. But choosing a subject for an epic is much more like choosing a wife: in either case it is pretty much a choice for life. Don't hurry it, therefore, the Renaissance critics said. And when you have chosen, still don't hurry: let it work in your mind. At last it will come to you, and life will seem to stand still while you write it. Even then, no haste; and when it is done, be slow to publish. Horace's advice was good. Immortality is what you aim at, and immortality will not be rushed.

Could a more lifelike account be given, in as many words, of the procedure of Milton? After the first delights of Travel have abated, and the applause of the Italian Academies which he frequented has a little died away, he is revealed, while still abroad, in his true character, as an epic poet in search of a subject. Shall it be King Arthur? or what shall it be? And shall it be in Latin (the language of educated Europe) or in this remote English Tongue?

No sooner is he home than the search is continued—more systematically. History and the Scriptures are ransacked—his reading now is the reading of a practitioner—and a long list of topics is noted—still surviving in his own hand in that Trinity MS. I spoke of, ninety-nine in all, including among them no less than four distinct sketches of a possible *Paradise Lost.*

The years passed, and they were years not as Milton had

expected them; but though little of the great poem was
written, during the Civil War and Commonwealth, it is
difficult to suppose that it was ever forgotten. It was growing,
and shaping in his mind—the one great stillness in that
storm of controversy: growing, while, as he says, 'the brick-
bats flew.' When he settled to compose it at the age of fifty,
i.e. about 1658, the scheme, the cosmogony, the theology,
the characters, and possibly even some of the great speeches
of the poem, were, I believe, already formed in his mind.

I must not dwell too long on his Italian journey. It has
been well related, and its details are known. He was hailed
in the Italian Academies as a prodigy—which indeed he was:
for once, let it be recorded, Academicians were right. What
learning! And so handsome, with his auburn hair, and his
girlish complexion of the north: *non Anglus*, *sed Angelus*, they
said, as if the remark were quite new. It is astonishing how
much we know of his visit. The Academies kept minutes;
and then there are those amateur detective agencies, Visitors
Books. So that we know how, on 30th October 1638, 'Mr.
John Milton, with his servant' (for he travelled with a man)
dined at the English College in Rome. In the Album of
another house we detect him again, in June 1639—in Geneva,
on his way home. He had been asked for some verses, and
he wrote two mottoes: the first, from the end of his own
Comus: the second a Latin tag, which was far from being a
tag to him, and was less so now than ever:

'Caelum, non animum, mutant qui trans mare currunt.'

The best translation of this is his signature in the same album:
Joannes Miltonius Anglus—'John Milton, these travels notwithstanding, an Englishman still.' But he never forgot Italy,
and the hills of Fiesole or the pleasure of that time. All his
life he looked back on it with a particular fondness, and
cherished every memorial of it. They gave him presents, and
he kept them religiously: even the MS. of fifty amorous and
not quite proper sonnets dedicated to him by their friendly
author, Antonio Malatesti. 'The memory of you, Jacopo
Gaddi,' he writes in 1652—fourteen years afterwards, observe,

when so much had happened to obscure such memories—'the memory of you, Jacopo Gaddi, of you, Carlo Dati, of you, Frescobaldi Coltellini, Bonmattei . . . is still delightful to me, and such as time shall never destroy.' None of these were great men. They were merely gentlemanly, and witty, and kind; and that is a great deal. It is good to see Milton thinking so.

He has been much misrepresented, surely. He was not naturally a grudging man, or a sour man, as is commonly supposed, though blazing and bitter enough in controversy. Youth, and ease, and gaiety, and the disinterested kindness which we call good manners were at all times pleasant to him, and he was himself a good companion. 'Extreme pleasant in his conversation, and at dinner, supper, etc.,' John Aubrey notes even of his last years.

Milton wrote little while he was abroad. The only piece of lasting interest is his Latin epistle to Count Manso. His three Latin epigrams on the singer Leonora Baroni, whom he heard at Rome, only tell us, what everybody told her, that her singing was divine. They were three drops in a shower: a book was made of her praises, in five languages. If only Tasso's Leonora had been *this* Leonora, says Milton, how fortunate for Tasso! He would never have gone mad—or, if he had, he would have enjoyed the luxury of being restored by her singing.

The hexameter Epistle to Manso is a very different affair. This fine old nobleman—the friend of Tasso and Marini—bred in war and courts, a poet and a scholar, now living among his own Neapolitans, suggests what Philip Sidney might have been, in old age, in Devon. He had been kind to the young Englishman, and Milton was always quick to respond to kindness. I am a pilgrim youth, he says, like Chaucer before me, from those lands of the pole-star (for so he describes this island) where genius ripens late. And yet, he would assure his host, the Thames is not without its swans. Lie though we may under the seven stars of the Plough—long though our nights may be—we English honour Phoebus and the Art of Poetry, and have done so since the

Druids. What the future may hold, I cannot tell: but this thought has come to me: to call up into song the old Kings of Britain—Arthur, still stirring there in the underworld, and the Knights of his Table—and shatter the Saxon phalanx beneath their charge:

O modo spiritus adsit
Frangam Saxonicas Britonum sub Marte phalanges!

(There is a line for you: it shows how much of the ring of poetry a summary conceals.)

Milton, we know, never wrote this Epic, or ever, I think, attempted it. If he had, we should have seen the splendid fragment: for he did not throw things away. But he was always attracted by the British story, and had been so from boyhood. Arthur and his Knights appear even in an undergraduate Latin exercise, in prose, on some totally unattractive and dissimilar theme, storming an enchanted castle. It slipped in, as the Fairies, in another exercise, make an equally unexpected entrance among the Predicaments of Aristotle. And to the end of his life they kept slipping in, even into the sacred Epic poems themselves. It has been supposed that Milton rejected the Arthurian Fable as having too little body of history to support an Epic: and that is probably true. An Epic is a solid structure, quite different from the bungalows of Romance. It is built to last and it should be planted on rock. Besides, the romantic Britons were going out, and—what has not been sufficiently noticed—after long neglect the Saxon was coming in. The Elizabethans had ignored the Anglo-Saxon heroes, but they were now to have their day. Their Church polity was studied by our English Church Reformers, in search of national precedents, and their Civil polity, their Parliaments, with the same motive, by the constitutional Reformers of the Civil War. The change came in Milton's time, and there is no doubt that he must have been aware of it. The romantic Briton fell out, the Norman was minimized, and the Anglo-Saxon took the place in our national history which, with occasional perturbations, he has occupied ever since. The great book on the matter, which

the Commonwealth swore by, and which Charles II pro-
hibited, was Nathaniel Bacon's *Historical and Political Discourse of the Laws and Government of England . . . with a vindication
of the Ancient Way of Parliament in England* (1647). It is the first
ancestor of Green's *Short History of England*, and that lauda-
tion, somewhat high-pitched and not now so fashionable as
it was, of the old English Freeman, and the Witenagemot,
the mother of Parliaments.

Milton returned to England, as he tells us, because of the
Troubles, and shortened his tour on that account. He was
ashamed to travel in search of culture when his country was
in difficulties. He had known long enough that trouble was
coming; the terrible warning in *Lycidas* to the hirelings and
ignoble pontiffs of the Church was neither sudden nor unpre-
meditated. He had refused to enter the Church of England
six or seven years before for very much these reasons. He had
seen good men exiled, his old tutor among them, and in an
early epistle to him, written in his eighteenth year, had
deplored with much feeling the intolerance of the Anglican
establishment and the Star Chamber tortures. Dr. Johnson
took the liberty of jeering at Milton because he did nothing
more, when he returned, than set up school and resume his
studies: but he does not suggest what else, if anything, he
might have done. It is plain that in returning to England
Milton designed no action more immediate or patriotic than
the return itself; to be at hand, i.e. among his friends, if
wanted. He watched, and listened, and waited (for freedom
and England were the same to him), but for some eighteen
months he taught his boys and thought of poetry and heroes.
The hour for action struck soon enough.

One disaster he had suffered while he was abroad—not
easily overstated. It must be reckoned among the chief misfortunes of Milton's life that, at the time, perhaps, when he
most needed him, he should have lost his closest friend: the
only one of his contemporaries with whom he was completely intimate. They were of the same strict principles, but
Charles Diodati carried his lightly. He had neither Milton's
intemperate abstinence nor his intolerance of shortcoming.

I think in the same way of Shelley, that other passionate Republican and Universal Reformer, deprived, not by death, but by distance, of the mild and playful wisdom of Thomas Love Peacock. Milton, when he settled in London, was driven upon his own thoughts, or into the one-idea'd company of Puritan controversialists: Smectymnuus, (you know the monster) that pantomime horse of Puritanism, with his old tutor, back from Hamburg, the Rev. Thos. Young, as its performing hind-leg. Milton was meant for better company: he needed gaiety, and good-humour, and such talk as he had got in Italy, the unembarrassed talk of artists, and gentlemen, and poets. I fancy he got very little of these things, and I welcome the more eagerly the solitary indication that he got them at all. 'Once in three weeks or a month,' says his nephew, 'he would drop into the society of some young sparks of his acquaintance, whereof were Mr. Alphry and Mr. Miller, two gentlemen of Gray's Inn, the beaux of those times. . . . With these gentlemen he would so far make bold with his body as now and then to keep a gaudy-day.' Diodati, I am sure, both as friend and as physician, would have held out for once a week—for the study in Aldersgate Street was 'hard' and the diet 'spare.'

Milton's elegy on Diodati—the *Epitaphium Damonis*—is the last of his important Latin poems: and it is the best. It is a pastoral, no doubt; and therefore, as Dr. Johnson reminds us, fictitious; but what it really says is Truth, and has the excitement of Truth. Milton had heard in Italy of Diodati's death, but, as he tells us, he could not feel the full force of it till he got home, and sat once more 'beneath the accustomed elm-tree.' Then the thing came over him, and first: How terrible to die so young—without a name! The same cry is heard in *Lycidas:* what if he were to die like this, *he*, John Milton, with nothing done! Milton's ambitions were deliberate; but the fierce and smouldering passion which inspired them blazes to the sky in such places as these.

He was really, this time, heartbroken: it doesn't matter about Edward King. 'What faithful companion will cling to me now, like this old familiar friend . . . who is there now

F

that I can trust with all my thoughts? With what friend now shall I cheat away the long evening sweetly, with chat by the fire, while the roasting pear hisses in the ashes and the chestnuts crackle, and the south wind bellows confusion without, and thunders in the elm-tops?'

This is a picture of Milton, and of an English winter evening—how English it is!—which we could ill spare; and it is too little known. If it seems unMiltonic, what are the odds that we have misunderstood Milton? You may see his snuff-box in a case in the Bodleian; he was a smoker also, and took wine, and when a lady sang sweetly in his presence, he said, though he was blind, that he knew she must be beautiful, to sing like that. The acrid visionary of the common portraits seems not at home in these surroundings. There is a passage in one of Shelley's letters which I am fond of, and which I put in my mind with that fireside piece of Milton's. He is writing to Peacock, and an impulse comes over him to describe his ideal English home—he, the exile, the Universalist, to whom privacy and domesticity, like patriotism, was logically a solecism, a selfish error:

'The shrines of the Penates are good wood fires, or window-frames interwined with creeping plants; their hymns are the purring of kittens, the hissing of kettles; the long chats over the past and dead, the laugh of children; the warm wind of summer filling the quiet house, or the pelting storm of winter struggling in vain for entrance.'

If this is unlike Shelley, what is the chance that in some important matter we may have misunderstood him also? Note the luxury of these poets, as they paint their snug felicity: the wind, for both, must howl outside.

But all the great poets of England have felt like this. Neither exile, nor the tyranny of principle, can divorce them from this love of home, and of their country.

We should read the *Epitaphium Damonis*, with its memories of friendship, of long winter evenings, and long summer days together in the grass, of talk and laughter 'while the heavy Rustic snores under the hedge.' (This Rustic seems to have made a great impression on Milton: as if he had half admired the perfect grossness of his ease. He snores in one of the early academic exercises, also, and in *L'Allegro*.) Girls are named, and in particular one girl from Essex : there are a great many girls, it occurs to us, in Milton.

The poem is full of memories of Italy, which he had meant to share with his friends ; and grief cannot prevent them from being very pleasant memories. All his presents : he had meant to show them—and just, perhaps, a little ludicrously, because he had so keenly looked forward to that moment—he describes at great length what death had prevented Diodati from seeing—Manso's two cups and so on. The truth is, Milton was still so full of the excitement of his travels that even his genuine grief is coloured and infected by it. He is very human, this Milton.

The poem has a remarkable close. What can he do—what can be done—to make up to Diodati for all he has lost—dying in the bud and first blossom of life. Certainly he is in Heaven : for he was pure. He is among the heroes and the everlasting gods, quaffing ethereal chalices, and drinking the joys of the blessed. This is uncommonly like Valhalla. But there is more. Diodati is to be further compensated, and in a manner more Oriental than Northern. He was young, and strong, and pure, and unwedded. There are special honours for such as he. His head shall be crowned with a golden garland, and waving green branches of palm he shall walk in the glad procession, acting and repeating for ever the endless heavenly nuptials, while the song never fails, and the lyre and the dance mix to madness, and the revel rages, and the thyrsus of Sion beats time to the Heavenly Orgy!

The poem ends : and we ask ourselves what kind of Heaven is this? I know nothing to equal it in any Christian poet for sensuous and pagan audacity. The thyrsus of Sion! Dr. Johnson objected to the mixture in Milton of Christian and pagan imagery on solemn subjects, and found fault with *Lycidas* on that account; but he seems to have missed the Bacchanalian Paradise of the *Epitaphium*. Edward King is also provided for in Heaven; but his compensations are mild to the compensations of Diodati. I must leave the reader to interpret this: and to surmise further, how much of Milton's abstinence and purity was due to an iron will. 'One cannot read without a smile,' says Mr. Bradley of Wordsworth, 'his reported statement that, had he been a writer of love poetry, it would have been natural to him to write it with a degree of warmth which could hardly have been approved by his principles and which might have been undesirable for the reader.' That smile has somewhat faded by now: Wordsworth meant what he said. Milton might have made an even stronger statement; and Mary Powell, his first wife, could have confirmed it, as indeed it is sufficiently confirmed by Raphael's blush.

The *Epitaphium Damonis* would have been singularly unMiltonic had it contained no reference to his poetical ambitions. Something had come over him the other day: what did it mean? 'My pipe has been sounding strangely lately: sounding strains of an unknown strength. Only twelve days ago I was playing, and my pipe flew apart—the music I played was too bold and grand for it.' It is another announcement, in the symbolic pastoral way, of the heroic poem to come; and an announcement, also, as he makes it, that his poem shall be in English, and not in Latin: that he has abandoned the foible of European fame. I shall be content, and think it distinction enough, though not a soul abroad shall ever hear of me:

> If only yellow-haired Ouse shall read me, and the
> drinkers of Alan Water

> And whirling Humber, and the groves of Trent,
> And Thames, my own Thames—she, above them all,—
> and yellow Tamar of the mines,

> And the far-off wave-washed Orkneys—if those shall
> con my lines, I shall be content.

It seems an odd debate to us: whether a man, having something important to say—and still more, to sing—should say or sing it in Latin, or in his native tongue. But every serious writer in Europe had been faced by it, in some degree, for centuries. Milton, to this date, had used Latin in his writings almost as much as English; and the applause of the Italian Academies had revived an old ambition. But I cannot think that the debate was ever real, or the decision in much doubt. *Really*, this debate had been settled at Horton: if not actually in his nineteenth year, in that address to his Native Language, when he burst through the forms of academic decorum, and deserting the Latin, in which he had begun to speak, astonished the assembly with some English verses.

> 'Hail, Native Language, that by sinews weak
> Didst move my first endeavouring tongue to speak.'

There, even then, was his true fidelity.

It was a sacrifice, of course: for English was harsher than Latin, and less moulded for song. I change the Latin music, he says in the *Epitaphium*, for the British screech: the skirl of the Britons. This northern harshness was an old reproach, of which Milton was no doubt reminded in Italy; but I doubt if the author of *Comus* took it very seriously. There is a time in the history of every language when its rawness is apologized for; and one must not be surprised when old reproaches turn up, quite out of date: for old reproaches never die.

Milton studied the resources of the English language as they have hardly been studied since. He has creamed, for those early poems, our poets from Chaucer to Drayton. He is sometimes blamed for being too learned in his diction; and at other times for introducing to a smaller race of men, in the next century, the gilded curse of poetic diction. But no poet of his time dug deeper in his youth in the authentic language of our native poetry; or did more, by his example, to establish it for future poets. Dingle, and bushy dell, and bosky bourn: I take one handful: his early poems are packed with these English riches, and they were preserved by robbery: for the eighteenth century poets found they could live on them. They might not know what *dingle* meant, and they had the pleasure of finding out; *dank* also was puzzling, and many others: but they all were used.

> 'banks with osier set
> That only prosper in the wet,'

85

says Fletcher in his *Faithful Shepherdess*. 'Osier dank,' says Milton in *Comus:* and the thing is done in two words.

But I must not wander among these felicities. I should think Milton, within his range, the greatest master of poetical epithet in the language.

And so I leave him, a full journeyman of his great Art, content with these British Islands as his world.

FRANCIS BACON AND THE REVIVAL
OF ENGLISH HUMANISM

IT was the habit of the French when they would introduce us to the characteristic opening temper of their seventeenth century to hand us a volume of Montaigne. There was a time, which lasted long and may come again, when, as an introduction to the mood and temper of the English seventeenth century, we should have been offered, with no less certainty, a volume of Francis Bacon. Both those gifts are, in my opinion, eminently suitable, though, in that same line of thought, we should probably add to the English present the works of John Donne the poet, something of Burton, and a little of Sir Thomas Browne. The reason is that the same ultimate problem troubled and possessed them all. The great question of that century, not only in England but in Europe, the question which controls the 'ondulations' of Montaigne and the impatient optimism of Bacon, which fires Donne to despair and smoulders in the humorous melancholy of Burton, which is at the root of Browne's *Vulgar Errors* and throbs in the most exalted musings of his *Religio Medici*, was the disputed extent of human ignorance and human knowledge. How much did we really know? How much can we ever know? And when these questions had been answered, if they were indeed answerable, how were we to comport ourselves accordingly and patch up a truce with faith? Very different answers were given and very different conclusions were drawn from them as to our consequent behaviour. But on one point there was fairly general agreement, and that was that we knew for certain extraordinarily little.

It had been supposed, for example, for a millennium and a half, that the earth was the stationary centre of a finite universe, and that the sun went round it. It was now asserted, and indeed proved—though the majority of thinking men, with Bacon among them, refused to be convinced—that the earth was not the centre of a finite universe, but only one among innumerable revolving bodies in a vast immensity of space. Nor was it stationary, but revolved about the sun.

It is very difficult now to imagine the shock of those assertions, of this terrestrial dethronement, to learned and devout men; for 'the new philosophy' hit both learning and religion. It was the pride of the Catholic Middle Ages to have forged into one system the Ptolemaic and the Christian universe, and so compactly riveted them together that one, it seemed, could hardly fall without the other. It was a wedding, as tight and fast as a learned Church could make it, of science and religion.

We cannot wonder, then, that Copernicus, the Polish Canon, concealed his discovery of the revolutions of the heavenly bodies until the year of his death, and only published by entreaty in 1543 what he had discovered thirty-five years before; or that his successor, Galileo, continued to teach the old errors from his Chair in Padua, and delayed his revelations until the appearance of a new star in the year 1604 set all the heads of Europe shaking, and supplied him with a text.

I do not know, I have not examined just what appearance that star makes in French literature and journals, but the reader will find it all over the literature of that time in England. He will find it in Bacon, in Donne, in Burton, in Browne, in Ben Jonson. Everyone talked of it, and drew, or shrank from drawing, his own conclusions from it.

It was not, indeed, the first occurrence of the kind. In 1572, when Bacon was a young student at Cambridge, a new star had appeared, as bright as Jupiter, and had then most preposterously gone out. It was hoped that it would be the last of its species, that Nature would recollect herself and relapse into her preordained decorum. Yet here, within a generation, was another!

One may ask why there should have been all this fuss. They should have been interested and pleased. They were certainly interested. For, by these two extravagances of

Nature, yet another cherished belief had been upset. It was an axiom of the Christian astronomical theology, and had been an axiom for centuries, that the Firmament is Unchangeable and Incorruptible; and here were these very heavens suddenly lighting up, and presently extinguishing, in the very region of the Immutable, one new star after another, protesting by signs and wonders against a cardinal doctrine of the old natural philosophy, which was also, by incorporation, the doctrine of the Christian Church.

Is it surprising that on these, as on other grounds, some men turned sceptics? (How do we know that we know anything?: that infinitely reiterated question of Montaigne's.) Or that some had already turned reformers of method, like Bacon? For clearly, if real knowledge be possible (and he believed fervently that it was), the true method had not been found. Or that others, like our English Burton, turned amused and melancholy spectators, watching men 'run, ride, turmoil, and macerate themselves'—for what?: he, meanwhile, 'laughing at all,' but with a smile a little twisted? Or that yet others, such as John Donne, turned revilers of the world, bitterly disillusioned to find their science thrown away and all the proud interpretations of man, together with that magnificent centrality of his, crumbling, perhaps, into words and fable?

> And new Philosophy calls all in doubt,
> The Element of fire is quite put out;
> The Sun is lost, and th' Earth, and no man's wit
> Can well direct him where to look for it.
> And freely men confesse that this world's spent,
> When in the Planets and the Firmament
> They seeke so many new; they see that this
> Is crumbled out againe to his Atomies.

Donne turns with contempt from a declining world to the pitiful spectacle of human impotence:

> In this low forme, poore soule, what wilt thou doe?
> When wilt thou shake off this Pedantery,
> Of being taught by sense and Fantasie?
> Thou look'st through spectacles; small things seeme great

Below; but up unto the watch-towre get,
And see all things despoyl'd of fallacies:
Thou shalt not peepe through lattices of eyes,
Nor heare through Labyrinths of eares, nor learne
By circuit or collections to discerne.
In heaven thou straight know'st all, concerning it,
And what concerns it not, shalt straight forget.

The despairs of great poets are never valueless, even when they seem least helpful; but Donne, the anti-Baconian, parts company here from the best hopes and prospects of his century.

Francis Bacon, like John Donne, was born and bred in one century, and came to maturity in another. He grew up in the reign of Elizabeth, but reached greatness in the early seventeenth century under a very different sovereign, King James I. How, in these respects are we to place him? Here we are met by a very odd practice of English literary historians — I mean, their habit of extending the term 'Elizabethan' to cover almost the first forty years of the seventeenth century.

When a political historian speaks of the Elizabethan Age, we know what he means. We understand him to refer to that period of time when Elizabeth in fact was queen, and that is what he does mean, because he is an honest man. Pick up, on the other hand, any literary manual or lecture syllabus of this period, and you will probably read 'The Elizabethan Age 1557 to 1637': which is odd: because Elizabeth was not yet queen in 1557, and by 1637 she had been dead thirty-four years. Of course I know how it is done; you know how it is done; we know the game. There was a certain rather mediocre, though historically interesting, Tudor Anthology of Verse called *Tottel's Poetical Miscellany*, which came out in 1557, and in the appalling barrenness of that time, and because the young Elizabethans read it, must somehow be got in, though it is not an Elizabethan book at all. And then, Ben Jonson the dramatist dies so very invitingly—*ultimus Romanorum*—the 'last of the Elizabethans'—in 1637, just before the curtain fell, in the Civil Wars. One sees the temptation, and *how* it is done: but *why* is not so easy. For there are dates about, and dates are sturdy things.

The situation is even more singular, really, than I have represented: because we find that, of Elizabeth's long reign, it is only the last twenty years or so that are at all 'Elizabethan' in this special literary sense. When literary lecturers or critics are attempting to be interesting about what is called 'The Elizabethan Age,' this is where they begin to glow: and even then only very moderately: about the year 1579 or 1580. Before that date, in the reign of Elizabeth, any subject, indeed, for literary enthusiasm would be hard to find. We are left, then, with this strange result that of the effective literary Elizabethan Age the greater part is in another Age altogether: the Age of James and Charles: another Age, and as most of its writers knew, and some of them to their cost, a very different Age.

It was Coleridge who started (as he started so many other things) this epithet 'Elizabethan' on its grandiose and devouring career, and gave it this wide and impressionist meaning. He came to these authors as to a new and unmapped country, and could not be expected to be very particular about boundaries. Those were the days when it was still possible to speak of 'one Marlowe.' Reading in this tumultuous exploring way, and contrasting these authors with their successors of the age of Dryden, with their new lightness and ease and their modern dread of being dull, Coleridge and his friends saw the earlier race quite naturally as one great family or dynasty—the Titans of Elizabeth. King James and King Charles and all that their names stand for historically—everything, I mean, that was particular to their age—seemed to Coleridge, in the sight of literature, so many political accidents—knots in the ancestral and overshadowing Elizabethan oak. It was a fine sweeping notion, not altogether devoid of truth, and was notably aided by the overmastering interest of our English nineteenth century in Elizabethan drama, and by the undeniable and admirable fact that the dramatic tradition created in Elizabeth's reign, and very near the end of it, had a fine, clean and distinguished run of some fifty years. Anyhow, Englishmen were soon talking familiarly of the 'Elizabethans', whom they had been taught to regard as a race artistically and almost divinely extended a full generation beyond the Queen from whom they took their name. This is a theory—an impulsive and attractive theory—of literary descent and inspiration. It implies that such works as *The Advancement of Learning*, for example, which Bacon presented to King James in 1605; Ben Jonson's *Volpone* and *Alchemist*; Burton's *Anatomy of Melancholy* (1621); even Milton's *Comus* (1634) and Browne's *Religio Medici* (1642) are so much nearer to the literary spirit of Elizabeth's reign than to the spirit of their own or of any other age that they must be classified, exceptionally, not by chronology, but by affinity.

Of such writers as Bacon, and Ralegh, and Ben Jonson, Elizabethans born, something on these lines might, no doubt, be maintained: but we must discriminate. The spirit of the Jacobean and Caroline times was very different from that of Elizabeth, and in some important respects antipathetic to it. The clouds are lower under the Stuart Kings. There is a drop in temperature. 'A certain heaviness of mind,' it has been said, 'natural in men who feel that they are committed to a huge task with no clearly foreseen issue, is observable in all the greater and graver literature of King James's reign. It is perhaps not fantastic to connect Shakespeare's tragedies [and the searching, searing scepticism of so much of his later work] with this atmospheric change. The confident morning temper of the later sixteenth century passed away, and the only gaiety that remained was the gaiety that is first cousin to recklessness.' There is a sentence of Bacon in his *Novum Organum* (I. 104) which comes to the mind as almost a Jacobean motto:

Intellectui non plumae, sed plumbum addendum et pondera.

('Let the Intellect shake off its plumes, and weight itself with lead.')

It is the passage from the Elizabethan to the later age: the plumes are gone, and toss in the wind no more.

It is, also, yet another of Bacon's challenges, to himself and the new century, to complete the half-finished work of English Humanism: to take up, however late—and he was bitterly conscious how late it was—England's delayed and divided Renaissance. Literature had been advanced in his time, but not learning or scholarship with it. We had had in England our Revival of Learning, like other countries, but it had been meagre, brief, and abortive, stamped out, when it was just beginning, by the brutalities of a monstrous King and the disorders of religion. Of all this, though he stood so much nearer to it and had not our advantages of perspective, Francis Bacon was magnificently aware, and, though he dared not say so, must have known why these weightier tasks of Humanism were still to do in England. We killed our Humanist leaders. When Lord Surrey was executed, there went the best poet of his day, one who might have founded a school which would have lasted a generation and filled those sterile spaces which now daunt the literary traveller through the first twenty years of Elizabeth's reign. When Sir Thomas More was beheaded, there died a martyr and our first English Humanist. 'Had Erasmus,' it has been said, 'instead of being an honoured guest at Rome, at Paris, or in the States of the Empire, been beheaded by Charles V or Francis I, all learning would have felt the blow and shrunk.'[1] When Sir Thomas More died a shudder went through Europe, and learning in England did literally shrink and wither.

We cannot wonder, in the face of that grisly story, if over the succeeding reigns of our English sixteenth century there hangs an air of exhausted vitality. A nation must pay for having a Henry VIII; new life could not well grow in that shadow. It was from these cold fields that Elizabethan England grew, and the growth was slow, slow and incomplete. The first things to revive, as flowers will mask and beautify a battlefield, were all the bright and natural and instinctive things. After long stillness, a sinister stillness, poetry lifted up its head and then there came in a blaze Spenser, Shakespeare,

---

[1] *Blessed Thomas More and the Arrest of Humanism in England:* J. S. Phillimore, *Dublin Review*, 1913.

and their fellows. But it was, as Bacon said, a semi-barbaric splendour. The Elizabethan Age produced one supreme, and many good poets; for a barbaric people may still produce great poetry. But the English nation had still to be humanized to complete the task of its civilization.[1]

That all, or most of this, was clear to Bacon, and to him above all Englishmen of his time, I cannot doubt. I would found, indeed, almost his chief claim to distinction on that fact. He speaks often of the loneliness of his studies and speculations, and indeed, to explain his mission, and the eleventh-hour fervour of his preaching, we must go back behind the Elizabethans altogether. The intellectual ancestors of Francis Bacon are hardly to be found in Elizabeth's time: but if we go back a little further, and look in on Sir Thomas More and his Socratic circle in Chelsea, we shall find some of them there, and something also of his inspiration. Of direct inspiration we have indeed one noted proof, though I do not wish to make too much of it; for our two greatest Lord Chancellors, More and Bacon, have each portrayed an imaginary commonwealth of mankind. Bacon's *New Atlantis*, that attractive and very personal sketch, in which the Royal Society of the future, for the advancement of science, is depicted in what seems an almost laughable glory of purple and fine linen, when one thinks of the professors one knows, was evidently written with More's *Utopia* in his mind, however different his own targets.

Bacon, who once commanded, in the Latin tongue, a European audience, is now chiefly read in English, and above all in his *Essays*, in his *Advancement of Learning*, and in that interesting fragment of scientific fiction which I have just mentioned. What a fortunate thing it is when a Reformer and Visionary, whose business is to make us dissatisfied, can offer us also the luxury of a style! Whatever we may think of some of Bacon's visions, or of some of his public actions, pen in hand he is never less than admirable and in the class of the magnificoes. I can think of no better lesson in the graver sorts of English composition than to observe by what arts of

[1] See J. S. Phillimore.

sober enrichment, with Montaigne and Seneca in mind, Bacon has expanded his original ten little essays—very bald and dry—into the fifty-eight which we read to-day. That first starveling issue—there were three editions, and we read the third—that first starveling issue, he said, was like 'the late new half-pence which though the silver were good, yet the pieces were small.' As he worked at them, in snatches of time—these 'dispersed meditations,' as he called them—the pieces grew larger, their ring more melodious, and to the silver he added gold.

One character they have which has never in England failed to excite applause: I mean their masterly way of opening: nor is there anything so tell-tale of a good writer; so, for that matter, is a good ending; only, having got so far, one hopes the end will take care of itself. It is the beginning which intimidates, when all is still to do. 'Good writers, like good violinists,' said Walter Raleigh, 'can almost be known by what is technically called their attack, the beautiful precision and clarity of their opening movements.' Raleigh used to relate with delight and approval the story of a Glasgow Professor of last century, who, though a Scot, professed the English language. When his students handed him an essay, he never altered his formula. He asked them with a great air of affected benevolence: 'Have you remembered to strike out the first page?' The advice may strike us as rough and ready; it is nevertheless good advice. I suppose that one reason for delay in getting to the point is the fear of what will happen to us if we say what has to be said and say it at once. The wisest course, I believe, is always to say it and run the risk: to begin with something real in the well-founded hope that one real thing will breed another. The best writers practise this directness. 'I was a great solitary when I was young,' says Stevenson, and *The Pavilion on the Links* has begun.

It is an interesting exercise to look at the opening lines of poets. I find Milton, in England, easily the most secure. There is a great deal of uncertainty, however, even among our greatest geniuses of the romantic revival of last century. There is a sonnet of Keats on Chatterton which begins,

> O Chatterton! how very sad thy fate!

Keats had not really got going, and was faced, moreover, with the dilemma of a proper name; he was wading in, and the water was still about his ankles. He takes the plunge in the second line, which he ought so plainly to have made his first, throwing away the other when it had done its menial work:

> Dear child of sorrow—son of misery!

The poem is launched.

I have produced nothing so far to prove the finality of Bacon's openings. He is almost as infallible as Milton. I will give only a few, out of many, from his *Essays*.

Of Gardens:

> 'God Almighty first planted a garden.'

Of Marriage and Single Life:

> 'He that hath wife and children, hath given hostages to fortune; for they are impediments, to great enterprises, either of virtue, or mischief.'

Of Parents and Children:

> 'The joys of parents are secret; and so are their griefs and fears: they cannot utter the one; nor they will not utter the other.'

Of Superstition:

> 'It were better to have no opinion of God at all than such an opinion as is unworthy of him.'

Bacon had at his command enormous resources of eloquence: but no man of eloquence was ever more chary of using it. He was aware that there are very few occasions in life which really call for eloquence. He always determines just how much passion the situation will warrant, and allows himself something less. We can all practise his directness of aim, if not his majesty.

The *Advancement of Learning* was published in the year 1605, about the end of October. It was just four or five days before the real Fifth of November, the fated Gunpowder Plot. And here was Bacon, making up little parcels of presentation copies, writing charming little aphoristic letters to the favoured recipients, and quite especially packing up and addressing a copy to the King. No one, least of all the King, found any chance of looking at the book for a very long time. One may say, and it would be true, though heartless, that such a book could afford to wait. It could, but not its author. Its author was tired of waiting; he had been working and waiting all his life, and at forty-five years of age, when a man ought to be settling down, Bacon was still without any public office, and in his studies still solitary and unencouraged; he could wait, he felt, no longer.

There is one remarkable feature about this book which the reader might not at first observe; it is not merely dedicated to the King; it is addressed to him, and addressed to him throughout. Bacon's immediate audience is not the world of readers, but King James. A Dedication normally follows the title-page, but the Dedication here is actually a part of the title-page and even of the title: *The Twoo Bookes of Francis Bacon, Of the Proficience and Advancement of Learning Divine and Human, To The King*. Each of the two books into which it is divided has the same heading or half-title; each addresses the King; and there is no breaking off to address ordinary readers at all. The King *is* the reader throughout. This is so very unusual with so large a work, that I believe Bacon began it as a private memorial to be shown only to the King and his friends. He was always writing memorials on projects and public questions; why not a memorial on the greatest project of his life? He expected great things from James, that singularly unsatisfactory monarch. The new reign was to be a new age, because the new king was himself a scholar. 'The canvassing world is gone,' he wrote, 'and the deserving world is come . . . I find myself as one awaked out of sleep.'

The First Book, 'a kind of inaugural lecture on the dignity and merit of learning,' is one of the great Defences—a Defence of Learning as illuminating in its kind as Sidney's *Apologia for Poetry*. It was begun almost on the news of James's succession, and was written with great care. It is one of his best compositions, and was in print before the Second Book was sent to press. This second book, unlike the first, was written hurriedly, printed hurriedly, and is in several parts unfinished. As usual he had spent too much time on the façade.

The general design of the two books was to state what had been done, and what still wanted doing, in all the fields of literature and science. They are a stock-taking of the past and a prospectus for the future. He dwells on the necessity of supporting researchers, and of bringing them into touch with one another, and takes a high view of the remuneration of professors—a view which I must think just, but which is still well ahead of present practices. I think he never really believed that he himself could do much more than draw the chart of this great humanistic advance. He knew that he was an amateur researcher. 'I shall be content myself,' he wrote to Lord Salisbury, 'to awake better spirits, like a bell-ringer which is first up to call others to church.'

The First Book, which deals with the *Proficience of Learning*, has, I think, a definite polemic intent. It is concerned to point out what human industry and science, against all disadvantages, had in fact already achieved. I take it to be in one regard Bacon's answer to the sceptics, the shoulder-shruggers, the second-hand Montaignes of the age, who laughed at science because some of its oldest beliefs had recently been bruised and shattered. It is his answer also to another and often more deadly sort of sceptic, I mean the godly sort, who saw in the disgrace of the old learning, the Copernican exposures and the rest, one more proof that we should abstain from impious curiosity—leave Nature alone, give up prying into her secrets, into second causes, and throw everything on that Eternal First Cause, which we worship as God. The most distinguished and most eloquent representative of this faction was, in that generation, John Donne, and I quoted earlier his sincere statement of disillusion—false science had betrayed us, and John Donne also, and must not therefore be forgiven. He turned in disgust from human learning, and advocated, in all earthly and material things, agnosticism for the glory of God. Against that attitude, which I shall always forgive when it produces poetry, but not otherwise, all modern science is a protest, and a triumphant protest. Bacon wrote in a time of doubt, and his chief glory is that he never doubted, and foretold this triumph. The crippling antithesis which the religious set up between first and second causes, and the works of God and man, he refused to accept. The end of knowledge was to reconcile them. '. . . as if there were sought in knowledge,' he said, 'a couch whereupon to rest a searching and restless spirit; or a terrace for a wandering and variable mind to walk up and down with a fair prospect; or a tower of state for a proud mind to raise itself upon; or a fort or commanding ground for strife and contention; or a shop for profit and sale; and not a rich storehouse, for the glory of the Creator, and the relief of Man's estate.'

The main purpose of the *Advancement of Learning*, which was his most influential book, Bacon must be held to have achieved. He drew, as he believed, the Map of human knowledge, and marked the waste places. Some of these, he had hoped, might be cultivated in his lifetime, and even by himself: he was sanguine about that, and over-sanguine about his special Method. But he knew, when he drew it, that the filling of those deserts in the Chart of Science was to be, for the most part, a long-drawn-out work for Posterity.

Two of his demands were answered within that century. He had asked for a Collection of Popular or Vulgar Errors about the natural world, and, with a view to invention, for a History of the Mechanical Arts. These projects, because he had named them and was revered, became two of the principal employments of the century. Sir Thomas Browne did the first, in a book which is not without amusement, and the Royal Society, which was to recognize him as its Patron and sit under his portrait, did the second, and indeed attempted both.

Bacon, in the last hundred years, has lost his high position in the ordinary speech and opinion of England. He has been ungratefully derided by modern scientists, who are usually so much better equipped for the study of the present than of the past. I say ungratefully, because amateur as he was, and over-ambitious, he wrote their State Papers for them, in the great interregnum when Dogma was crumbling, and Knowledge, for a moment, was actually afraid. He thought of himself as a discoverer, like Columbus, sailing into the unknown; though all that he could do was to dream and plan the voyage. Yet it was something to do that, and to plan it in such noble diction, in diction which was to have such dispersion among mankind. Of the genuineness of his visions there can be no doubt. His thought rings with passion, though the full ecstasy of real scientific discovery he was never to know: such ecstasy as Kepler's when he formulated in the year 1618 his third law: 'that the squares of the periods of the revolutions of the planets are to each other as the cubes of their mean distances from the sun.' That species of perfect and rounded satisfaction was denied to Bacon.

'It is now eighteen months,' says Kepler,[1] 'since I got the first glimpse of light, three months since the dawn, very few days since the unveiled sun burst upon me.' He is referring to the above formula which, I am sorry to say, conveys nothing whatever to me. 'Nothing holds me'; he goes on, 'I will indulge in my sacred fury . . . I have stolen the golden vases of the Egyptians to build up a tabernacle for my God—far away from the confines of Egypt. If you forgive me, I rejoice; if you are angry, I can bear it: the die is cast, the book is written, to be read now, or by posterity—I care not which: it may well wait a century for a reader, as God has waited six thousand years for an observer.'

This is the true Poetry of Science. Here if anywhere is the right answer to the disillusionists: something for which Bacon, in a good moment, would have surrendered both his title and his Chancellorship: for it is the ecstasy of truth, and the truth of original discovery.

[1] *Harmonices Mundi*, 1619.

SIR THOMAS BROWNE

IT is the distinction of Browne that he combines a sceptical irony with an undamaged religious temper, and the new courage of the Baconians and experimental science. Alone of all the writers of his time he was able to join the *meditatio mortis* and the philosophy of human vanity with a cheerful and truly scientific and undismayed pursuit of knowledge, and to round his piety with an art of life as delicate and nicely ordered as Montaigne's.

Though the 'Religio' will probably always be the most popular of Browne's works, and though the 'Urn-Burial' (which would now be a paper to an archaeological society) is probably his finest piece of writing, there is truth in Professor Saintsbury's remark that 'an appreciation of "Pseudodoxia" is the real touchstone of appreciation of Browne generally.' We see better here than anywhere just what he had to work in, and how he worked. All sciences are involved, and theology, the architectonic science, with them. Modern specialism had yet hardly appeared, or that progressive alienation of one science from another and of all science from literature of which the ill consequences were never more candidly acknowledged than to-day. The *Pseudodoxia Epidemica* is, in the first place, a Baconian book; an explicit answer to one of Bacon's requests, when he asked for 'a calendar of popular errors,' such errors especially of natural science as 'pass in speech and conceit, and are nevertheless detected and convicted of untruth.' 'As things now are,' says Bacon, 'if an untruth in Nature be once on foote, what by reason of the neglect of examination, and countenance of Antiquity, and what by reason of the use of the opinion in similitudes and ornaments of speech, it is never called down.' The First Book of the 'Pseudodoxia,' on the causes of common errors, is a deliberate expansion of Bacon's sentences in the 'Advancement of Learning.' It all began in Eden, apparently, this very human tendency to error, in that famous interview with the Serpent; and Browne tells Eve, a little late, what she should have said.

'Whoever will be cured of ignorance,' says Montaigne, 'must confess it.' This is the hardest part of Knowledge, that it must be made, as Browne puts it, 'by oblivion'; that 'to purchase a clear and warrantable body of Truth, we must forget and part with much we know . . . impartially singling out those encroachments, which junior compliance and popular credulity hath admitted.' He wishes that the task of surveying this vast territory of Error had not been left to one man, complaining, like Bacon, in spite of his numerous correspondents, of intellectual solitude and the lack of 'co-operating advancers.' Added to this are the disturbances and interruptions of his profession, so that he must write in 'snatches of time,' as medical vacations and the importunity of patients allowed. His readers who enjoy 'quiet doors and unmolested hours' will deal gently, then, with his short-comings; for 'a work of this nature is not to be performed upon one leg.' Like Bacon, he is aristocratic, and writes not at all to Tom, Dick and Harry, among whom he includes the dolts and timber-heads of all classes, but to the ingenuous gentry of England, and 'those honoured Worthies, who endeavour the advancement of Learning.' He does not try, therefore, to be plain and easy, in the later Royal Society manner: 'the quality of the subject will sometimes carry us into expressions beyond meer English apprehensions,' and often into 'the America and untravelled parts of Truth.' Yet in the second edition he made things easier, dropping many technical words and quotations in the original languages, and in other ways consulting the convenience of his countrymen.

The greatest enemy of Knowledge, he declares, is the Goliath of Authority and received opinion, and the inbred feeling that the older a statement is the nearer it approaches to the fountain of truth. It was generally allowed by thinking men that we knew little for certain, that most of our opinions were taken upon trust; but they differed about the remedy, and even doubted, some of them, if any remedy were possible. ''Tis not amiss,' says Montaigne, that our opinions are hereditary, for 'we could not choose worse than by ourselves in so weak an Age.' Browne believed, like Montaigne and many others, that the world was in its decline, and pitied the populations of 'three or four hundred years hence, when no man can comfortably imagine what face this world will carry.' But while he lived he tested authority in all seemly matters, and preferred the evidence of his senses to the word of Aristotle. Aristotle puts the problem, for example, in his book on animals, 'Why a Man doth cough, but not an Ox or Cow?' But oxen and cows do cough. Exit, therefore, Aristotle on Cows! They even cough when in health, as Walter Scott maintained before Lord Eskgrove in one of his first cases at the Edinburgh Bar. But the Judge would not have it: 'A coughin' cow!—that will never do—sustain the Sheriff's judgment, and decern.'

There are many old favourites among the questions and 'popular tenents' that Browne investigates, and he cannot conceal his pleasure in them even while he explodes them. What is the cause of thunder?—the fool's question in *Lear*. Is gold in physic a cordial, as Chaucer declares? What about the eagle-stone? A friend of his in Iceland shall tell you; though, as to the virtues popularly found in stones—whether precious stones or others—'he must have more heads than Rome had hills' who can make them out. Are there mandrakes that scream, that 'shriek upon eradication'? Many plants, no doubt, make 'a small and stridulous noise' upon divulsion of their parts; such a noise we observe when we pull up a parsnip. Exaggerate this, and you have the mandrake's scream. Few ears have escaped the noise of the dead-watch, the

> little clickling sound heard often in many rooms, somewhat re-
> sembling that of a Watch; and this is conceived to be of an
> evil omen or prediction of some person's death; wherein not-
> withstanding there is nothing of rational presage or just cause
> of terrour unto melancholy and meticulous heads. For this

noise is made by a little sheath-winged gray Insect found often in Wainscot, Benches, and Wood-Work, in the Summer. We have taken many thereof, and kept them in thin boxes, wherein I have heard and seen them work and knack with a little *proboscis* or trunk against the side of the box, like a *Picus Martius*, or Woodpecker against a tree. It worketh best in warm weather, and for the most part giveth not over under nine or eleven stroaks at a time. He that could extinguish the terrifying apprehensions hereof, might prevent the passions of the heart, and many cold sweats in Grandmothers and Nurses.

Here is simple observation and experiment such as not all the sceptics were willing to apply. It is characteristic of Montaigne, says Sir James Stephen, that his scepticism never extends to matters of fact. He repeats the advice of sportsmen that, if you want to find out which is the best worth keeping of a litter of puppies, the way is to carry them off from the kennel and keep the one which the mother first brings back. It never occurs to him to ask how, when all the rest are drowned, you can possibly tell that the one so chosen was the best. Browne would not have passed this; any more than he will accept the very common assertion that the brock or badger 'hath the legs on one side shorter than the other.' If we survey the animal world, 'we may in their legs, or Organs of progression, observe an equality of length and parity of Numeration.' So the basilisk is put in the dock and outstared, and it is proved by experiment that the King-fisher hanged by the bill, does not, by any 'occult and secret propriety,' show in what quarter the wind is. The griffin and the phoenix are dismissed like the basilisk. He bred toads and found no jewel in their head. He saw no reason to believe that a peacock is ashamed when he looks on his legs, though common belief will have it so; nor that the lion fears the cock; nor that it is good to be drunk once a month. This last, he declares, is a common flattery of sensuality, supporting itself upon some of the known healthful effects of inebriation. Perhaps his best experiment is that of the toad and the spiders, of whose combats and poisonous destruction of each other 'solemn stories have been written.' His report is that,

Having in a Glass included a Toad with several Spiders, we beheld the Spiders without resistance to sit upon his head and pass over all his body; which at last upon advantage he swallowed down, and that in few hours, unto the number of seven. And in like manner will Toads also serve Bees.

His reluctance to dismiss these vulgar errors too speedily, his pleasure in playing with them, is apparent everywhere, and very plainly when he comes to the elephant, 'whereof there generally passeth an opinion it hath no joints.' He dwells a little on this notion, and how, 'being unable to lie down, it sleepeth against a tree.' Is not standing more tiring that walking? he asks. No animal could long survive this perpetual extension of its muscles. Besides, 'we have had the advantage in England' of seeing an elephant both kneeling and lying down. He could not bring himself to put this first and so break the matter off.

Browne lived in a troubled age, an age of informers, persecution and civil war; but his excellent temper, his unworldly tastes and the privileged character of his profession carried him safely and honourably through. He has been idly pictured by some injudicious and merely literary admirers as a kind of gentle Norvicensian Diogenes, 'shutting his study door' against the quarrels of his time, and shaming the drums and trumpets of his countrymen. But a busy doctor, of course, cannot shut his door like this, as indeed he tells us, or his ears either; and Browne never pretended indifference to the quarrelsome politics of his day. He was one of 432 citizens who in 1643 refused to subscribe money for the parliamentary recapture of Newcastle; and after the Restoration he had the Royal Arms elaborately carved over the mantelpiece of his drawing-room. He bred a sailor son, and followed his fortunes in action like any other father so proudly circumstanced. He was, in fact, however he might retire himself in thought, much warmer-blooded than some of his admirers allow, and understood better, also, both the duties of a citizen and the nature of courage. Though the company of soldiers can never at any time have been greatly to his taste, he recognizes, like Dr. Johnson, that mystery of the sword which would make us ashamed to follow Socrates and hear a lecture on philosophy if Charles XII at that moment called for volunteers to dethrone the Tsar.

> The heroical vein of mankind [he writes] runs much in the Souldiery and couragious part of the world; and in that form we oftenest find men above men. History is full of the gallantry of that tribe; and when we read their notable acts, we easily find what a difference there is between a life in Plutarch and in Laertius.

Here, with the same humility, is Dr. Johnson's observation. This lofty habit of action has other consequences; its field is not only the field of battle:

> Where true fortitude dwells, loyalty, bounty, friendship, and fidelity may be found. A man may confide in persons constituted for noble ends, who dare do and suffer, and who have a hand to burn for their country and their friend. Small and creeping things are the product of petty souls . . . Pityful things are only to be found in the cottages of such breasts; but bright thoughts, clear deeds, constancy, fidelity, bounty, and generous honesty are the gems of noble minds; wherein, to derogate from none, the true Heroick English Gentleman hath no peer.

2

The Miscellany Tracts and Letters of
Sir Thomas Browne

The 'Miscellany Tracts,' first printed in 1683, are letters sent in answer to the inquiries of correspondents, among them such notables as Evelyn and Dugdale. Thirteen manuscript copies are extant, and from these Mr. Keynes[1] has drawn variant readings and some additional passages. The bulk of the fifth volume, however, consists of memoranda, loose papers and note-books of Sir Thomas, preserved by his son and now in the British Museum and the Bodleian. . . .

It is pleasant to turn the pages and read where one will

---

[1] *The Works of Sir Thomas Browne*, edited by Geoffrey Keynes.

among these interrogations and projections of Browne's rich
and questing mind. Nothing comes amiss to him in nature or
in art; his curiosity is insatiable, and what the scientist in
him rejects the antiquarian rescues. All questions are approached with the same ripe and methodical gravity. He
discourses with equal interest and satisfaction of the Fishes
eaten by our Saviour, of Cymbals, of Garlands, of Ropalic or
Gradual Verses, of Artificial Hills, Mounts or Burrows, or of
the Oracle of Apollo. The slenderest topic in his hands
acquires the composure and the dignity of ordered knowledge. One is impressed by his zeal both as observer and as
experimenter. He was a great collector; and if a strange bird
or fish were caught in the neighbourhood, or any mineral or
antiquarian oddity found, our Norwich doctor was sure to
hear of it. Many of his queries have the quaintness, as we
think it, of their period; but queries no less quaint may be
found in the early *questionnaires* of the Royal Society. No
question in natural science was then felt to be simple, since
every step in natural knowledge had to be retrod. 'Why a
pig held up by the tayle leaves squeaking,' 'Whether the
heads of all mummies have the mouth open, and why,'
'Why solipeds or whole-hooft animals arise with their fore-
leggs first, bisulcous with their hinder,' 'Whether till after
fortie dayes children though they crye weep not, or, as
Scaliger expresseth it, *vagiunt sed oculis siccis*'—this random
list had its counterpart, no doubt, in many notebooks of that
time, when the Baconian 'advancers' had got at last to work.
Now and then he leaves his queries and collections, and lets
his mind play awhile with mysteries. There is a fragment on
Dreams which might have slipped out of almost any of his
published works:

> Half our dayes wee passe in the shadowe of the earth, and
> the brother of death exacteth a third part of our lives. A good
> part of our sleepes is peeced out with visions, and phantasticall
> objects wherin we are confessedly deceaved. The day supplyeth
> us with truths, the night with fictions and falshoods, which
> unconfortably divide the naturall account of our beings. And
> therefore having passed the day in sober labours and rationall

enquiries of truth, wee are fayne to betake ourselves unto such a state of being, wherin the soberest heads have acted all the monstrosities of melancholy, and which unto open eyes are no better than folly and madnesse.

Much may be gleaned by the biographer from these miscellanies. Browne, we learn, kept an eagle two years, 'which fed upon kats, kittlings, whelps and ratts, without one drop of water.' He liked making verses, both in English and in Latin, and transcribes some of these efforts with a certain pride. 'Being in the country,' he will note, 'a few miles from Norwich, I observed a handsome bower of hony suckles over the doore of a cottage of a right good man; which bower I phancyed to speak as followeth'; and he copies out the Latin lines. There are admonitions in the commonplace books about prayer. Seven times within the twenty-four hours it was his duty to call upon God. He would pray in all places where privacy incited. So that there should be no street or passage in the city of Norwich which might not witness that he had not forgotten God or his Saviour in it; and he would take occasion to pray upon the sight of any church which he might see or pass by as he rode about. The conduct of his life, it is clear, was more to Browne than any ambition as a writer or even as an advancer of knowledge.

Browne was happy in his wife and family, in Dame Dorothy and his sons and daughters; and no volume in this edition is more welcome than the sixth which contains his private and domestic letters. Of the 232 letters eighteen are to his second son, Thomas—'honest Tom'—a fine lad whose promise of a distinguished career in the Navy was cut short by his early death. His father thought the world of him, and his letters show a touching solicitude for his welfare. When the boy goes to France on his travels, at the surprising age of fourteen, he is followed by the most assiduous instructions about his demeanour and studies. He must be courteous and civil to all, but 'put on a decent boldness'; he must keep up his Latin, and practise his French, take draughts of all notable buildings, and observe the rarities of nature wherever he goes. Tom, for his part, delights his father by sending home 'pritty stones and insects' for his collection. He is last heard of in letters in May 1667, being then twenty years of age, and seems to have died that year.

Of the other family letters 142 are to Sir Thomas's elder son, the physician Edward, and four to his daughter Elizabeth. In the letters to Edward the affectionate relation of father and son is blended with that of the senior to the junior practitioner. They certainly reveal Browne as a hard-working and most conscientious professional man. Edward, coached by his father, and enlightened by travel, became a prominent London physician, and they were evidently very proud of him at Norwich. But the paternal advice did not cease. Be careful and frugal, the old man writes; be temperate at feasts—'no such pitiful thing as a Guttling': take heed that tobacco 'gayne not to much upon you, for the great incommodities that may ensue, and the bewitching qualitie of it which draws a man to take more and more the longer he hath taken it': write your letters 'at the best advantage, and not when the post is ready to go': and spell not 'sceleton with a k.' Sir Thomas himself economized where he could, in time and in words. Indeed he goes farther in plainness than even these modern days allow, with his D.S. for 'Dear Son,' and his subscription 'Y.L.F. T.B.'

His closest friend among his daughters seems to have been Betty. There is a note in Volume V of 'The books which my daughter Elizabeth hath read unto me at nights till she read them all out'; and there follows a portentous list of some twenty-six or more folio volumes, mostly travels and history, besides 'some hundreds of Sermons,' and ' many other books, treatises, discourses of severall kinds, which may amount unto halfe the quantity of halfe the books in folio.' The books, it is true, were in English, but even so the poor girl almost enters the class of Milton's daughters. Like her sisters she could draw, and sends Edward a sketch of a stork 'taken by the sea side and brought a live to my father; it was so pretty a one I could not but take the Picture . . . ; it is about a yard hye and the tamest stately thing that ever you saw.' The Brownes were all given to keeping animals; we hear of Sir Thomas's hedgehog as well as his birds; and Edward, a little later, was keeping an ostrich in London.

I have said nothing of Dame Dorothy and her grandson, 'little Tomey,' though they are the best known and the most engaging features of the Browne correspondence. We first hear of Tommy in 1677, in a postscript by his grandfather; he was 'lively God bee thanked,' he tells Edward, and 'when wee send away our letters hee scribles a paper and will have it sent to his sister, and sayth shee doth not knowe how many fine things there are in Norwich.' By 1678, Tommy being boisterous, they are having 'sober stayd little girles for his playfellowes that hee maie imitate them.' Presently Dame Dorothy takes up the tale: 'Tomey is very well: goes to scolle and is a very good Boy and delights his grandfather when hee comes home.' A year passes and Tommy craves for manhood. 'I hope you thinke of Tomey's Briches against the Assise,' she writes to her daughter-in-law; 'he growes a brave tall boy and will be much a Man if wee have but Briches.' June comes to an end, and 'Tomey would give all his stock to see his Briches.' Fourth July, and 'Tomey much longing for his briches': 5th July, the briches are come, and Tommy 'much delighted and sends . . . dutty and thankes, and promis to war them carfully.' For five years this thread of news runs on. Now Tommy is a little fevered, and looking 'as though something would break out'; or he is so active that his grandfather is 'fayne to hire him to sit still half an howre'; or he has gone to see two bears, or wants, says his grandmother, 'a Tumbler for his popet show, a punch hee has and his wife and a straw King and Quen, and ladis of Honor, and all things but a Tumbler which this Town cannot aford, it is a wodin fellow that turns his heles over his head.' The correspondence ends in June 1682, with Tommy still well. We know that he became a physician, like his father and grandfather; but there history and biography give out.

ST. EVREMOND

A GENTLEMAN of France, bred in camps and courts, a soldier, wit, and epicure, St. Evremond, before he came to England as an exile, had been one of the ornaments of that brilliant, vivacious, and turbulent society which has given to the Regency of Anne a special character in French history. He was also one of the first to feel the change of temperature at the new Court of Louis XIV. For reasons never, I think, fully explained he incurred displeasure, and in the year 1661, being then a man of forty-five, at a time when he might reasonably have expected further advancement, he was banished the kingdom. The sentence held against all the entreaties of his friends, influential as these were, and when it was at length recalled, a quarter of a century later, he was too old to do anything about it or even care very much. His long life was thus almost evenly divided between active residence in France and involuntary idleness abroad, an idleness consoled by the pensions of successive English Sovereigns, and tempered and made tolerable by good living, which he understood in its last refinement, by good talk, of which he was equally a connoisseur and a practitioner, by the pleasures of literature and music, and, in short, by all those nicer satisfactions which lie open to a man who enters without question the best society of whatever capital he may choose to inhabit. The capital he was led to choose was London— one of the three genuine capital cities of the world, he said. He had his home there for nearly forty years, and dying at last in the conscious pride of nonagenarianism (a mistaken pride, as the gruffness of modern research has discovered), he was buried in the nave of Westminster Abbey, near Chaucer and Spenser and his friend Cowley. A visitor to the Abbey may survey his bust, of which his friends approved the resemblance, and, if he will consent to climb a ladder, may also read the obituary record of the old man's life. It is for one half of it, as I have said, the life of a soldier and a wit, two vocations less inclined to be incongruous when every gentleman wore a sword. Condé and Turenne, we read, had approved his valour in the field. *Relicta Patria*, the legend proceeds—sinking that troublesome business of the banishment in a very absolute ablative—*relicta Patria, Hollandiam, deinde a Carolo II accitus Angliam venit*. He came (what Frenchman *did* not come when Charles invited?)—he came, and, as the inscription records, was honoured and familiarly known by English Royalty and the first circles of an English society, cultivating throughout his years among us philosophy and polite literature, and both in prose and verse enriching his native tongue. This distinguished man, the epitaph concludes, is to be ranked and remembered among the leading writers of his age.

Contrary to the law of its species this epitaph does not lie. Only in one forgivable particular it tries the conscience: his verses, for the most part, are beneath regard.

It might be opportune to present some picture of a life which in so pointed a manner brings France and England together, and to examine a reputation for which his native and adopted countries would seem to share, in some degree, responsibility. St. Evremond in his time was the most distinguished representative of French manners and polite learning in foreign parts. He was also the first Frenchman of distinction to transmit to our continental neighbours an intelligible account of at least a portion of our island literature. Not only in the trade of gossip and the casual exchanges of friendship, but in the more important traffic of ideas, St. Evremond, during the greater part of his residence among us, was an unaccredited but influential ambassador between the two nations. In numerous communications he even confirmed the view, already tentatively held in France by the more forward-looking spirits, that good sense and *l'esprit* were actually to be found beyond the Gallic frontiers.

My own interest in St Evremond began many years ago when as an undergraduate I had the temerity to write, and even to publish, a historical essay on the Fronde. In that chaos of public and private interests I happened to come across this young Guardsman, as he then was, and noted the interesting and lively company he kept, his attractive gift of raillery, and his highly precocious sense of the Art of Living. I observed also, how steady a course he steered through the confusions of that time, and how nicely he had penetrated their folly. I might have guessed of course, from so much shrewdness, that he was a Norman—which means, according to Professor Saintsbury, 'a parcel-Englishman,' and may account for some of the ease with which he later accommodated himself to England. He was one of six brothers of an ancient Norman family, was originally destined for the Bar, and to that end had received an excellent education at Paris and Caen which opened the Roman writers to him, and enabled him (as has lately been discovered) to write in old age two Latin letters to Isaac Vossius, one of which contains a very creditable pun. But the wars were too enticing. When he was sixteen years old he deserted the Law and turned Ensign, served in Italy, on the Rhine, and in the Low Countries, had his company at twenty-five, and was distinguished among his fellow-officers, 'no less,' we are told, 'by his wit and elegance than by his courage.' For twenty-seven years he was employed in one campaign or other, rising eventually to the rank of Maréchal de Camp, and his service ended only with the general Peace of the Pyrenees. He had had his mishaps: some reported witticisms on the great Condé had cost him his command in that Prince's Guards: a too lucid critique on the government of Mazarin had landed him for a month or two in the Bastille: he had fought a duel, and found it convenient to withdraw to the country. But on the whole—except for a wound at the Battle of Nordlingen which was to give him trouble in England thirty years later—his affairs had gone well enough.

The only direct record of his campaigning is a poem of Bois-Robert's, written in 1645, of which St. Evremond's biographers seem not yet aware. It is addressed to Celidamant, whom M. Maurice Cauchie, the editor of the *Epistres en Vers*, has rightly identified with St. Evremond, and the occasion was the wound I have mentioned. The first news was of his death, and the Court was in despair. Then that he was alive, but permanently crippled. *At last*, the truth, and the prospect of a convalescent leave in Paris.

'One advantage, my dear friend—this wound will give you leave, and I shall be able to see you. What fun! How we shall laugh and live content! The ladies, never fear, will love you. And when it rains, we'll go—after a good dinner—to the play. We'll look at the latest books—by some member of that Academy you are so fond of. . . . We'll read by that roaring fire in your rooms; play cards; drink; and tell stories. We'll get in Castelmore to join us.

> Bref, au foyer rostissant la chastaigne
> Nous bastirons cent chasteaux en Espagne.

Then, little outings, if your doctor allows: good restaurants: *and* concerts—which, I know, please you as much as the finest verses.'

This is normal enough for a wounded officer on leave, but pleasing by its familiarity and friendliness. The ladies—the concerts—the play—the good dinner—the stories, and that roaring fire—all fit the St. Evremond we know.

Fortunately the campaigning of those days observed the course of nature, and winter, as a rule, saw St. Evremond in Paris, free to pursue the far from contrary pleasures of the table and the mind, and to unbend, if he chose, upon the softer passions. There is every sign that he left *none* of these opportunities unused. He went much into society, enjoyed life, read a little and wrote a little, and began to indulge a very formidable power of satire, which might have made him, in other times, the terror of ministries—the Swift of France.

'That Academy you are so fond of,' in Bois-Robert's poem, recalls the first of St. Evremond's pieces to find its way, I think, to print: a satirical comedy on Richelieu's new Academy, and its prentice attempts to purge and purify the language. Bois-Robert was himself one of the Academicians

satirised, but had evidently forgiven his fellow-Norman.
St. Evremond had presently better work to his name. He
experimented, like everybody else, with the fashionable
forms, of portrait and conversation, and one at least of these
performances—the inimitable discourse of the Maréchal
d'Hocquincourt with Le Père Canaye—remains a masterpiece of realism, universally judged as worthy even of Pascal.
He never again quite recovered this power, and the emptiness
of exile killed it.

Of his affairs of the heart he was too efficient to let us
know what does not concern us. But what he never tried to
hide was his devoted attachment to that astonishing woman
—peculiar flower of the 'bon temps de la Régence'—Mlle.
Ninon de l'Enclos. It was an attachment which lasted their
lives, long-lived as they both were, and ripened into one of
the kindest and most unselfish friendships in literature: I say
literature, because their letters to one another have a place
there.

Graver interests attached him to the famous Gassendi. He
emerged from these conversations a theoretical as well as
practical Epicurean, and easily converted Ninon to this congenial creed. The revival, in secular circles, of the philoso-
phical schools of the Ancients was one of the features of the
age. There were professed Stoics about as well; and Scarron's
father, in the time of Richelieu, practised the Cynic rule. The
fashion spread in a very original manner. Sir William Temple
reports in the next generation, that he had known, in the
family of a friend in England, 'a laundress firm in the
principles of Epicurus.'

It was in these years that St. Evremond made his first
acquaintance with the English Court, then in exile in France.
King Charles himself, the Dukes of Ormonde and Buckingham, St. Albans, Arlington and the rest, with whom he was
to live so intimately, were all known to him in Paris; Cowley,
too, he met, and Hobbes, whom he was to praise as 'the
greatest genius of England since Bacon,' and that eminently
kindred spirit, Waller. This lucky acquaintance he improved
as a member of the mission sent to congratulate Charles on

his restoration. He stayed nearly six months, and made, evidently, a conquest. When, some eighteen months later, the order of banishment went out against him, ostensibly as a punishment for some private invective against Mazarin and the Peace, a prompt invitation arrived for him in Holland to make the best of his way to Whitehall. There thus began for him that new existence, very slowly recognized as final, of an idle man in a foreign country.

Socially it was the easiest of transitions. When he moved to London he moved, as it were, *ad eundem*, taking his place in the Anglo-French circle at the Court. His mode of life, until the Duchess Mazarin enslaved him, was henceforth uniform. Whether in England or in Holland—to which he retired for five years on the approach of the Plague—he lived in Court and Diplomatic Circles, where French was spoken, and only strayed outside to make the acquaintance of some learned man. He had, for a courtier, an excellent catholicity. At no time could he wholly ignore the demands of his intellect. As he had sought out Gassendi in Paris, so he frequented Spinoza, the younger Heinsius and Isaac Vossius in Holland. He valued scholarship and learning. 'I do not look upon myself as anything,' he said, 'because I do not understand Greek.' If only the combatants in the Quarrel of the Ancients and Moderns could have embraced this sentiment, how empty and almost peaceful the battlefield! He liked men who knew about Books, and had a weakness for Royal Librarians. In course of time from among his scattered countrymen in London, he was to collect, for rainy days, a kind of dusty little Academy. Only there were two subjects in which he must not be asked to take an interest: Mathematics and Experimental Science. 'There are no commendations,' he says, 'which I will not bestow upon the mathematicians, provided that I am not one of their number.' As for Experiments, he had written from Holland, 'If I revisit England it will *not* be to see the Fellows of the Royal Society. I prefer the Duke of Buckingham's violin to his laboratory.'

England was to his taste. The climate, which wrecked one after another of the Ambassadors of France, suited him, on the whole, very well. 'What air! What verdure! Where can a man live longer or more insensibly grow old?' 'When there is next any question of filling the post of ambassador to England,' Cominges wrote mournfully home in 1665, 'the King will do well to cast his eyes on some broad-shouldered person.' St. Evremond had shoulders of the right size. Only, if the month of March might be abolished, and that English habit of putting greenery in the fireplace before the winter is gone. He has a poem on this: *Sur la verdure qu'on met aux cheminées en Angleterre.*

> Frais ornement de Cheminée
> Vous vous précipitez un peu.

Back to your marsh, don't return till June.

His old army friend, the Maréchal de Créqui (to come to higher matters), asked him, in due course, what he thought of English Society. His answer lifted the question. 'For these ten years past,' he replied, 'I have found as much pleasure, and been as happy in the enjoyment of conversation, as if I had been all the time in France. I have met with persons of as great worth as quality, whose society has been the greatest comfort of my life . . . I formerly thought [as de Créqui evidently still did] that there were no well-bred and polite men but in our Court . . . But experience has at length convinced me that there *are* such everywhere. . . . Every Nation has its excellence, with a certain turn proper and peculiar to its genius . . . In truth, the grounds of any essential quality are everywhere the same.'

In one of his tracts, the famous tract on English comedy, he comes closer to his subject, and ventures to distinguish the French and English character. He finds it the fault of the English that they dig too deep and lose themselves in the windings of their own thoughts before they can bring anything to the surface. 'They still dig when there is no more to be found.' The French, on the other hand, are too easily satisfied with surface effects and first results. 'It is as difficult for us to enter in as for the English to get out.' It would be good for each nation to learn from the other; for the English to acquire the art of human conversation; for the French to go deeper in their studies. In short, 'Les plus honnêtes gens du monde, ce sont les Français qui pensent, et les Anglais qui parlent.' It is his most famous sentence, and has the advantage both of being and of ringing true.

The social record of St. Evremond's life in England is to be found in his Letters, which are in many ways his most agreeable and interesting productions. Ninon in Paris used to read her letters from him aloud at her little salon, and one can readily see why. They recount a pleasant life, lived easily between town and country. When the Court moved to Windsor St. Evremond moved with it, living, I imagine, with his old friend Isaac Vossius, now oddly transmuted into a Canon of the English Church. And all over England, at Euston, at Boughton, at Clevedon or Audley End, or at Beaconsfield with Waller, comfort and friendship awaited him. His habit, however, was metropolitan, and he was always glad to return to the conveniences of a capital. 'Come to town, my Lord,' he writes to the Earl of St. Albans, 'the country was never made for such as you . . . A man of honour and politeness ought to live and die in a capital city. . . . This goodly and great City, called London, daily expects you; and here, my Lord, you ought to fix your abode. Free conversations at table, with a few guests; a game at Ombre at Her Royal Highness's; and Chess at home.' The call was unanswered, and he wrote again: 'Come! The Duchess of Portsmouth will give you what share in the Bank you please. My Lord Hyde . . . My Lord Ambassador . . . The Duke of Ormonde is ready to play with you at Trick-Track without odds . . . The Duchess Mazarin will even suspend her Basset for you. Mr. Waller has in store a delicious conversation for you.' As for St. Evremond himself he promises to play chess with him on Sundays, and lose! I hope this was answered.

St. Evremond's club, for a quarter of a century, was the house of the famous Duchess Mazarin, who, in 1675, pausing in her wildgoose cycle of Europe, was induced to settle on these shores. The unsavoury political purpose of this visit is well known: the Mazarin was to dispossess the Duchess of Portsmouth of the favour of the King. The scheme failed, because, I suppose, the Duchess Mazarin had not the Civil Service temperament. She claimed her right to fall in love when she chose, and did. St. Evremond, entranced by her vivacity, her beauty, her excellently run house, and admirable cook, installed himself as her admirer, and was so useful to her, in arranging her salon, conducting conversation, getting concerts up, and writing librettos and even music, that in the end she could not do without him. His letters are full of her tantrums, with forgiveness always at the end. I confess that some of these letters are disagreeable to me, though an attempt to make a list from them of the number of the Duchess's black pages and foreign waiting-maids, and of the tenants of the menagerie of birds and quadrupeds she harboured in her house, makes the correspondence less distasteful. In the end the poor lady died penniless and inebriate.

St. Evremond himself, now within sight of his ninetieth year, had by that time become a distinguished oddity, had grown careless of his person and, like his Duchess, kept a herd of animals in his house. 'Monsieur St. Evremond,' said Pope, [1] 'would talk for ever. He was a great epicure and as great a sloven. He lived, you know, to a great old age, and in the latter part of his life used to be always feeding his ducks; or the fowls that he kept in his chamber. He had a great variety of these, and other sorts of animals, all over his house. He used always to say that "when we grow old and our own spirits decay, it re-animates one to have a number of living creatures about one and be much with them."' The feeding of the ducks was almost an *ex-officio* act: for he had long held, under the Crown, the amusing and doubtless invented office of keeper of the Ducks in the Decoy in St. James's Park. Dick Steele remembered seeing him feed them.

Though his chief pleasure was in conversation there were times when even St. Evremond could not find a listener. To these oases of silence in a long and bachelor life we owe the

[1] Spence's *Anecdotes*, Section IV, 1734-36.

occasional pieces—the charming letters, the little essays, the parodies, and characters—which most characteristically preserve his name. There are certain subjects on which, as a moralist, he is more eloquent than at other times: on Friendship, above all, and on the proper management of Pleasure. He believed that 'it is more our interest to enjoy than to know the world,' but that 'in all our pleasures the mind should have a share.' There should be no hurry, or greed—no uneasiness, 'a thing tolerable in love only, when it is even pleasurable.' 'An imperfect enjoyment is attended with regret; a surfeit of pleasure with disgust. There is a certain nick of time . . .' The aim is serenity; and the happy temper, as in Epicurus, will 'desire without violence, hope without uneasiness, and enjoy without transport.' I am reminded by these injunctions of Dryden's remarks, that 'no heroic poem can be written on Epicurean principles.' Nor life lived. There is nothing heroic about St. Evremond except his desperate determination not to be defeated by Life.

Friendship alone can carry him away. 'Of all ties,' he says, 'that of Friendship is the only one that is endearing to me; and were it not for the disgrace of having my Affection slighted, I could love merely for the pleasure of loving, even where I should not be beloved again.' For this emotion he was amply rewarded in his life.

The history of his reputation is unusual, and the present state of it. It is not surprising that his repute has fluctuated, and that for the greater part of two centuries he has passed out of ordinary reading. If the world is lazy about him he was lazy first, and lazy on principle. He refused to regard himself as in the ordinary sense an author; never in his life sent anything to the printer; and manuscripts were scattered of which he had not even a copy. It was only in his last years, in the mood in which a man proceeds to tidy his affairs, that he was induced by his excellent, fussy Huguenot friend, des Maizeaux, to settle the canon of his works. No: what is odd about his reputation is that the critics are not yet agreed just what it is. He is praised for one thing in France, and for another thing in England. In France he is most regarded as a

moral essayist, to some extent, I fancy, because that fits him
so neatly into the manuals of French literature, on a shelf just
below those more celebrated performers in that field, La
Rochefoucauld and La Bruyère. In England, on the other
hand, he is most regarded as a critic, and has been named by
Professor Saintsbury as, after Dryden, the best critic of his time
not only in England but in Europe. This assertion becomes
even more impressive when it is found that the late Professor
Ker took much the same view. No such opinion seems ever
to have been held in *France*; what is surprising is that it seems
never to have been considered there. In only one branch of
criticism, and that not literary, has he secured in France this
sort of praise: his remarkable *Réflexions sur les divers génies du
peuple romain*. There undoubtedly, by one of those strokes
of native originality, of mere independence, which give his
work its savour, he showed the way to Montesquieu. But in
his *literary* criticism France, satisfied with Boileau, sees nothing
very remarkable. Now Saintsbury holds that St. Evremond's
Thoughts on French Tragedies is 'a piece of criticism which for a
contemporary of Boileau is altogether astonishing in the just-
ness of its sentiments and principles.' Of course we know what
Professor Saintsbury thought of Boileau. So of his strictures
on the French Histories of his Time, and his Observations on
Italian Opera, which contain the essence of all that has been
or can be said on the matter. 'I do not hesitate,' he says, 'to
place those three pieces of criticism above anything of the
kind which was written before the middle of the eighteenth
century, while the view which they express hardly obtained
general currency till the beginning of the nineteenth century.'
I should myself, if I had made that statement, have wished to
include the Critique on Racine's *Alexandre*. But I am afraid
that I swing here between the French and English view, and
am unable to subscribe to these high-pitched claims. I think
that St. Evremond was simply a superbly independent
reader, like FitzGerald, and every now and then said the
absolutely right thing.

Professor Saintsbury goes further, and in England sees St.
Evremond everywhere. 'In passage after passage,' he says, 'of

the great Queen Anne writers, his teaching and style are discernible. *The Conduct of the Allies* shows in point of style and flavour distinct reminiscences of the *Lettre sur la Paix des Pyrénées*. His characters and portraits foreshadow more clearly than any contemporary writings the great essayists of the decade immediately succeeding his death.'

I am afraid I can do nothing with this: for what is an 'influence'? I can neither confirm nor deny.

There are other claims on which I can throw more light. St. Evremond, like Dryden, with great respect for the Ancients, was on the side of the Moderns in that famous Quarrel, because he sided with the living and was for freedom; and a stirring picture has been drawn by critic after critic of St. Evremond's visits to Will's coffee-house, followed by his dogs, and of the very important discussions which he took part in there with John Dryden present. He 'led the vanguard in Temple's day,' says Spingarn; and could not possibly have thought so if he had known the truth. The truth is that we have all been hoaxed, and hoaxed by one of the most sober scholars of the nineteenth century.

St. Evremond was sometimes to be seen, says Rigault, making his way to one of those establishments recently founded in England, meeting-places of the nobility, men of letters, translators and index-makers in shabby clothes, ecclesiastics in cassock and bands, sprightly pupils from the Temple, and timid students from the universities. When he arrived, between Covent Garden and Bow Street at Will's coffee-house, leaning on his long cane, wearing his black skull-cap over his white hair, and followed by his dogs from which he could not be parted, because the aged, he said, had need of something lively near them, there was a pause in the conversation: respectfully the crowd would make way for him as St. Evremond walked through to the arm-chair where in winter near the fire, in summer on the balcony there sat in state a great man in snuff-coloured coat and curled wig, the glorious John Dryden. It was a privilege to pay one's respects to the illustrious poet, and to hear his opinion of Racine's latest tragedy or le père Le Bossu's *Traité du poème épique*. A pinch of snuff, offered by Dryden, Macaulay tells me, was an honour fit to turn a young man's head. St. Evremond would sit down beside the great poet, and they would talk of poetry, of the three dramatic unities, or discuss the question of the moment, the quarrel of the ancients and the moderns. In Will's coffee-house there was a faction for Perrault and the moderns, another for Boileau and the ancients. Sir William Temple would gracefully make fun of Perrault; Wotton would reply to Temple and call to his aid his formidable friend Dr. Bentley, who, charging into the discussion like a hoplite, routed the arguments of his foes. Swift, hastening to the assistance of Temple, threw into the fray, like a squadron of light horse, his witty epigrams, which rained on everyone, in particular on his cousin Dryden. St. Evremond would look on smiling at the encounter, then, when the heat of the controversy had died down a little, he would begin to speak quietly, reducing violent opinions to a more temperate level, and giving, through his moderation, to the cause of the moderns, an air of precision often missing in the arguments of Perrault and Desmarets.

One can see how it all arose. Rigault, fired by an animated passage in Macaulay's *History* on the rise of the coffee-house, was moved—however strangely—in his otherwise admirably business-like work, to practise fiction, to make a *Conversation*: and does it without a word of warning. Ever since, the critics and historians of literature have imagined St. Evremond as an almost daily visitor at Will's, taking part in the propagation of his critical ideas. In all probability the old man never set foot in the place, or propagated criticism beyond the private circle of his friends. Will's is nowhere mentioned by him. Dryden, of course, the monarch of Will's, knew all this very well and almost says so. 'Conversing in a manner wholly with the Court, which is not always the truest Judge, he has been unavoidably led into Mistakes, and given to some of our Coarsest Poets a Reputation abroad, which they never had at home. Had his Conversation in the Town been more general, he had certainly received other ideas on that Subject; and not transmitted those Names into his own Country, which will be forgotten by Posterity in ours.' [1]

That seems to me conclusive.

The result must be a general re-writing of most of the paragraphs on this matter in France and England, and a quieter but by no means less honourable station for St. Evremond himself.

How little he would have minded that! The man who said that to him 'eight days of life were more worth than eight centuries of glory after death.'

[1] *Miscellaneous Essays :* by Monsieur St. Evremond, translated out of the French. With a Character by A Person of Honour here in England. Continued by Mr. Dryden, 1692.

JOHN GALT

IT is a cause of complaint with many people nowadays that they cannot cross the threshold of a book without stumbling over the body of some editor or critic, planted there in the interest of his fraternity for the chastening of readers. The public grows tired of this mode of 'literary approach,' and has begun to count its bruises. I can well understand this. Yet there are purposes for which such dragomanship can never be obsolete. The world of literature is in this respect like the world of affairs, that it is a scene of constantly fluctuating reputations, where merit tends to obscure merit, and the applause of one age becomes the derision or neglect of the next. In such a restless competition of names it will sometimes happen, whether from bad fortune or from simple want of address, that the good man goes to the wall. This is the critic's chance; and criticism is never more useful than when it stoops to rescue obscured reputations, and to communicate to readers the forgotten intentions of authors. The *Annals of the Parish* belongs to a kind of composition rare in literature, and is almost supreme in its kind; but it is as little known to the present generation of English readers as the character of its author or the transactions of his life.

John Galt was born in 1779 at Irvine in Ayrshire, and was the son of a sea-captain. When he was ten years old his family removed to Greenock, and he was placed in course of time in a local house of business, where he remained until his twenty-fourth year. He liked the work, but from boyhood had maintained intromission with the Muses. The reading of Pope's *Iliad* inspired his first verses, a rebus on a limekiln; and Mrs. Radcliffe's *Italian* excited him to try his hand at tragedy. He became known in the west country in the Jacobin days as a Tory poet, and during the fears of French invasion helped to muster two companies of riflemen, 'the first of the kind raised in the Volunteer force of the Kingdom.' His mind at this time teemed with projects of advancement. He longed for success both in literature and in commerce, but was undecided which, if either, he should prefer. In this restless state he suddenly threw up his post at Greenock and migrated to London, where he entered into partnership with a young fellow countryman. Three years later, in 1808, the business came to grief, and Galt began that mixed career of literary and commercial adventure which he continued almost to his death. The puzzle of his life was how to reconcile these conflicting ambitions. In the next six years he was at one time or another law-student, researching historian, voyager, playwright and contrabandist; but the result of all this multifarious activity was not commensurate either to his hopes or to his exertions. His legal studies were soon dropped; his schemes for evading the continental decrees against our exports, which kept him travelling about the Mediterranean, ended in smoke; and of the three works which he published in 1812, his *Voyages and Travels* and his *Life of Wolsey* were reviled by Croker in the *Quarterly*, and his tragedies declared by Scott to be the worst ever seen.[1]

It was a discouraging start, but Galt was as obstinate as he was versatile. Putting aside for the moment his more ambitious projects, he took rooms in London, and sat down to write for a living. Nothing came amiss to him; he became familiar with every species of drudgery known to the literary hack, and found that acquaintance profitable. Biographies, books of travel, and articles on every variety of public question poured from his pen : he wrote without labour about what he knew, and where information had to be acquired his industry was untiring. One of his literary schemes at this time anticipated some ideas of our own day. It was a scheme for the publication of rejected plays, as a protest against the methods of the London Theatres; and such a collection in four volumes did actually appear between 1814 and 1815, with the eventual title of *The New British Theatre*. But its only

---

[1] Nevertheless, a later tragedy, *The Appeal* (1818) was performed at Edinburgh with a prologue by Lockhart and an epilogue by Scott.

effect, as Galt confessed later, was to vindicate the managers.[1] His projects, whether in literature or in commerce, never lacked a certain nerve: too often it was their only recommendation. For eight years he had been prevented by his literary employments from making more than occasional excursions into trade, yet he never lost touch with it. Even when he was writing hardest, he took pains to appear to the world as a man of practice and substance, and to cultivate the acquaintance of men of affairs. 'He had parliamentary friends,' says a Scottish observer, 'whom he well knew how to retain. He always appeared at his ease and independent, kept lodgings constantly in Downing Street, had great placidity and amenity of manners, and looked and talked very wisely.'

The turning-point in his reputation as a writer was reached in 1820, when he was forty-one years old. In that year he printed in Blackwood's new magazine his story of *The Ayrshire Legatees*. It was his first published attempt in that species of fiction in which he must be held almost without a rival. The plan was borrowed from Smollett's *Humphrey Clinker*, and the letters have much of Galt's peculiar humour; but the construction of the book is looser than the epistolary method could quite justify. Its success, however, was so great that he was reminded of a story which he had long meditated, and had indeed begun and nearly finished seven years before. This was the *Annals of the Parish*.

It appears that when he was very young, and still resident in Greenock, he thought of writing a book that might be for Scotland what *The Vicar of Wakefield* is for England, and early began to observe in what respects the minister of a parish differed from the general inhabitants of the country. The

---

[1] Byron about that time had the same experience: 'When I belonged to the Drury Lane Committee, and was one of the sub-committee of management, the number of plays upon the shelves was about five hundred. Conceiving that amongst these there must be some of merit, in person and by proxy I caused an investigation. I do not think that of those which I saw there was one which could be conscientiously tolerated. There never were such things as most of them!'

study, however, was not pursued with much energy, and the idea might have been abandoned altogether, but for the inspiration of a certain solitary Sunday walk which he happened to take through the neighbouring village of Inverkip. As he viewed the extensive changes in its appearance since his last visit, and moralized to himself on the nature of progress and the virtues of the old and new, his intention, he declares, of writing a minister's sedate adventures returned upon him suddenly, and he felt something like the glow with which Rousseau conceived his essay on the arts and sciences. Business and the common vicissitudes of life suspended the design for many years, but it was constantly remembered, and at last achieved. When the work was nearly finished he wrote to his old acquaintance, Constable the bookseller, telling him what he was about, but received no encouragement to proceed: Scottish novels, he was told, would not do. This, let it be noted, was in 1813, less than a year before the publication of *Waverley*; though, indeed, as Galt justly remarks, even had it been published, there was no resemblance between Scott's celebrated production and his own. Constable's advice was followed. The manuscript was thrown into a drawer and forgotten.

The private history of the *Annals* now draws to a close; and if at this point, surmising what is to come and remembering that other tale of *Waverley* and the fishing-tackle, the reader should make a moment's pause, let him admire the providence that thus presided over the double birth of Scottish fiction. Years after, having taken it into his head one Sunday to set his papers in order, Galt found among the rest the minister's chronicle. He looked it over, as an entire stranger would do, and thought it had some merit; a friend to whom he read some passages agreed in thinking it good. It was sent to Blackwood, and immediately published, in 1821. Once before the public, there was never any doubt of its success. It was received everywhere with praise. Scott, as we should expect, thought it 'excellent,' and Henry Mackenzie, the author of *The Man of Feeling*, whose long and wide experience of Scottish life peculiarly fitted him to judge, was enthusiastic over it in *Blackwood's*. Galt gave his readers no time to cool. In 1822 *The Provost* appeared, a composition, in the author's judgment, superior to the *Annals*, to which it was intended as a companion. It exhibits with great force, and by the same charming method of autobiography, the effect on a west country town of those movements which he had already shown at work on the rural life of Dalmailing. In the same year was published *Sir Andrew Wylie*, the most popular of his novels south of the Tweed, and in 1823 he wrote *The Entail*, which both Scott and Byron are said to have read three times! After the *Annals* and *The Provost* it is the best of his Scottish fictions; of the numerous works which he produced in the remaining years of his life not one comes near these three in merit. He began to aim at higher things, and was seduced by Scott's example into trying his hand at historical romance. The unmistakable failure of his attempts in this kind of writing must have disposed him to welcome even more ardently than usual an opportunity of active employment which offered about this time. In 1824 the Canada Company was formed, with Galt as Secretary, and as a Commissioner for Settlers' claims or as Superintendent of the Company he was to spend in Canada nearly three out of the next five years. His energy and ability were everywhere recognized, and in the virile joys of pioneering and the founding of settlements he seemed to have gained his heart's desire. But his old intractability was once more his undoing. He was headstrong and tactless; the lieutenant-governor could not endure him; and he was displaced. His return to England in 1829 only added to his misfortunes. He was seized and imprisoned for a debt of £80, long due for the tuition of his sons, and the worry and confinement broke his health. But though ill and in prison he continued to work with his old hardihood, and managed to compose a story of the American backwoods which had a considerable sale. Scott speaks of the book and of its author's misfortune in his *Journal* (11th July 1830). 'I have begun *Lawrie Todd*,' he says, 'which ought, considering the author's undisputed talents, to have been better. He might have laid Cooper aboard, but he lags far behind. No wonder: Galt, poor fellow, was in the King's Bench when he wrote it.'

From this time until his death in 1839 he was once more almost entirely dependent on what he could gain by his pen. His principle of 'easy writing' helped him. 'One of his favourite maxims,' says his Scottish acquaintance, Gillies, 'was that bookmaking being at best a kind of lottery chance, he could, by merely keeping the pen in his hand, begin and end a work in less time than a fastidious author would consume in laying his plans and debating how the thing was to be done.' At one time, we are told, he carried his principle so far as to finish no less than three romances of three volumes each in something under six months.

When Carlyle met him, in the beginning of 1832, at a dinner given by the proprietor of *Fraser's*, he was still free from paralysis, but had greatly aged. His friend and follower, D. M. Moir, who knew him in his prime, speaks of his 'herculean frame,' his jet black hair, and his piercing eyes. Carlyle's impressions, though hearty, were very different. 'Galt,' he notes in his *Journal* (21st Jan. 1832), 'looks old, is deafish, has the air of a sedate Greenock burgher; mouth indicating sly humour and self-satisfaction; the eyes old, and without lashes, gave me a sort of wae interest in him. He wears spectacles and is hard of hearing; a very large man, and eats and drinks with a certain west-country gusto and research. Said little, but that little peaceable, clear and *gutmüthig*. Wish to see him again.' From that year he suffered from repeated strokes of paralysis, and died prematurely in 1839, with a book of poems in the press. His life had been, in his own words, 'pinched with an inclemency'; and he had suffered, as it seemed to him, from the vice of a stubborn, ungainly integrity. Perhaps the passage in his life to which his mind most often reverted in his last years was his misadventure in Canada; and it is gratifying to know that he is still remembered there and that the reward denied to his labours in that country was successfully claimed by the merits of his family. Of his three sons, the youngest, Sir

Alexander Galt, became premier of the colony, and his second son, Thomas, a judge.

The most interesting thing about Galt is his thankless attitude to literature. When he was a very young man he believed, like many young men ignorant of the world, that literature was the first of human pursuits, and he was in love with 'the *post obit* halo that surrounds a literary name.' The change in his belief, as recounted in his memoirs, is of that dramatic sort which arranges itself so easily in the reminiscences of age. 'I was reading,' he begins, 'in the Lazaretto of Messina the life of Alfieri.' What he read there seems scarcely equal to the conclusion it was made to yield. He read that the greatest men are the men who have 'most benefited the world'; and his conclusion—the truth that 'descended on him like inspiration'—was that literature must always be held a secondary pursuit, the means merely of recording things done. Henceforth, he resolved, his aim should be, rather than to make books from topics supplied by others, to furnish a topic from himself. There is considerable force in this view of literature and action. It is in the cool assumptive manner of the notorious conquerors and reformers; but it wants such action to support it as was beyond his reach and powers. This was the whole trouble of Galt's life. The platitude from Alfieri was only the occasional and accidental cause of a determination from which his training and temperament and the circumstances of society left him no escape. The fervour of youth once past, he was a publicist by choice and an author only by necessity. It was thought by some people that in his *Autobiography* he had made too little of his literary reputation. But the truth is that he was not conscious of owing many civilities to his reputation as an author; he was even, it may be suspected, a little ashamed of being an author at all. The profession of letters was no longer the obvious avenue to preferment. Its hold on the practical imaginations of the day had been destroyed by the novelties of commerce. Even the complimentary phrase of the age, 'the ingenious author,' has a tell-tale sound. It is the comfortable man's praise of what in no way touches his interests, his tribute to a kind of dexterity in which he cannot imagine himself a competitor. We need not be surprised then, that writers who aimed at a public career took endless trouble to impress the world in some more solid and respectable character. Galt's lodgings in Downing Street, his principle of rapid composition and carefully maintained demeanour of burgher-like ease, were all moves in a game—the game which Scott and the whole Blackwood group of writers played so zealously in Edinburgh. They were meant to throw society off the scent, or to appease it by their evident contrition. 'All know,' says Goldsmith, 'that an author is a thing only to be laughed at . . . even aldermen laugh.' Now to be laughed at by an alderman was what Galt could never have endured. 'I shall not be justly dealt with,' he said, 'if I am considered merely as a literary man'; and he comforted himself with the thought that when his numerous books were forgotten he would still be remembered as the contriver of the Canada Company.

It is to these contending characters in Galt that we owe his best work; what is more, their contentions were never elsewhere reconciled. In the *Annals* and its companions the writer and the administrator for the first time worked harmoniously together. The end proposed was unusual in the fiction of his time. It was chosen in conformity to his notion of literature as the record of things done, and 'likeliness,' to use his own word, was the quality he valued most. He had a very sober idea of his proper talents as a writer; and it is amusing to observe how nicely his theory of literature is calculated to their measure. Nothing annoyed him more than to hear his west-country fictions spoken of as 'novels,' written for the entertainment of readers. They were not 'novels,' for they did not pretend to a plot; nor were they written chiefly to entertain, for they aimed at historical truth. Galt was never artist enough to be content, like Scott, with amusing his age, and he listened with impatience to the ordinary praises of 'invention.' The only legitimate sort of invention, he held, was that which consists in selecting and ordering the results of observation—in fact, the only sort of invention of which he was a master. Almost every page contains examples of the species of memorial congenial to him—'things of which the originals are, or were, actually in nature, but brought together with composition by art.' Cripple Tammy Daidles, known throughout the countryside for begging on a horse; the Major and Miss Girzie at the Breadlands, and the eccentricities of my Lady Macadam; the adventures at the placing of Mr. Balwhidder; the smuggling and the surreptitious tea-parties, are all drawn from the collections of the author's own experience, or from his grandmother's tales of life at Troon. Dalmailing itself, the imagined scene of these events, has a more than hypothetical existence. It is not simply any Ayrshire village. It has its place on the map. 'The scene is actually laid,' says Galt in his *Literary Life*, 'in the "whereabouts" of Dreghorn in Ayrshire. In a still evening I sometimes think of its beautiful church, amidst a clump of trees. . . . Nor is the locality to me uninteresting, as it happens to be the burial-place of my forbears.'

The *Annals of the Parish* was intended by Galt to be the Scottish *Vicar of Wakefield*, and the comparison is less unequal than might be supposed. Galt and Goldsmith have something in common: the turn of mind for such writing was natural to both. They have the same talent for the humours of simple life, and the same instinct for reminiscence. They are equally indebted for their material to the accidents of personal experience; and they have both an incorrigible fondness for copying from themselves. They are at home in the records of autobiography, and uncertain in the logic of plots. 'Any talent I ever possessed,' says Galt, 'lay in the direction of moral and visible description'; and he confessed that when he worked with a story it was always in galling harness. Goldsmith might have written these words of himself. If there is anything to complain of in the *Vicar of Wakefield* it is that the surprises are too patent, and the adventures disproportioned to the scale of feeling. The most dreadful events take place with such coolness of dispatch that we cease to wonder at the Vicar's acquiescence. We regard them as philosophically as he does himself. The fire that burned down the parsonage was, after all, we reflect, a very honest, punctual sort of fire, doing its duty by the author in the only way in its power; and young Thornton's wickedness a racy contrivance to give the girls a good run for husbands. We are soothed into admitting them as hypotheses. We do not submit to them as illusions. It is the simplicity and grace of the narrative, and the air of nature in the characters, that keep the book so fresh; the truth, in fact, of the 'moral and visible description.' The plot was never more than a perfunctory device 'to bring in fine things.'

The superiority of the *Annals* over the *Vicar of Wakefield* is that it does without hypotheses, and seems to do without illusions. To the interest of autobiography it adds the reality of a chronicle. Instead of confining his narrative, as Goldsmith did, to the private fortunes of a clergyman and his family, Galt hit on the excellent and original idea of presenting the sixty years of Mr. Balwhidder's ministry as a village drama with Dalmailing and Change of Circumstances for the protagonists. Mr. Balwhidder himself takes the double part of Expositor and First Villager, and American rebels and French revolutionaries figure in the background as the remote arch-villains, whose awful deeds, in accordance with classical precedent, are only reported in their consequences. The advantages of the plan are apparent. It saved the author from the dangers of an artificial plot, and gratified his love of realistic writing. His construction is borrowed, not from the stock properties of fiction, but from the orderly records of time; and he has the whole range of village humours at his command. Above all, he has introduced the minister in his proper character, as the leader of his flock. Goldsmith's plan gave him none of these opportunities. Dr. Primrose is never shown among his flock. His good words are chiefly employed upon his family afflictions. There is no village life; no schoolmistress, no precentor, no sexton, we might almost say no villagers. For though we come across a gentleman farmer or two, the real villagers never appear, except as a kind of stage chorus to the main action. They shake sticks and threaten the landlord when the Vicar is evicted. They cheer and throw up their hats when he returns in prosperity. It is a fine old English picture of the duties of society; but the Scottish view is more intelligent, and nearer to nature.

Galt showed good sense in his choice of time. The sixty years of the reign of Mr. Balwhidder and George III—for they undertook and demitted office upon the same day— were almost the first considerable period of settled order and security that Scotland had enjoyed for centuries, and they were employed to lay the foundations of her later prosperity. English travellers who had known the country before the suppression of the '45 could not conceal their astonishment at the profound change in its appearance and manners even twenty years after that event. The 'unripe fair' of Aaron Hill's verses gave up 'sighing at her sister's air,' and began to develop her charms. Her men of birth put down the sword for the plough, and assumed the farmer without flinging off the gentleman. Enlightened noblemen like Breadalbane and Lord Eglintoun encouraged agriculture and planting by every means in their power. The practice of the Lothian farmers was diffused over the whole country, and there came to be Mr. Kibbocks and Mr. Coulters in every shire. Even the smuggler forsook his doubtful romance, and took to the land.

In the credit of these improvements the nobles and gentry had naturally a principal part. But the advance in trade and manufactures in the last quarter of the century was the work of other classes. Coal-mines began it (there were three beside Dalmailing); cotton-mills and Cayennevilles inevit- ably followed. Decent unambitious men wondered if that could be for the best which so recently had seemed impossible. There were prophecies of strange mutations when a canal was proposed and actually begun between the Forth and the Clyde. In the meantime the stubborn class of small landed gentry stormed at the rise of the 'democraws' and the decay of privilege. For if trade, as Parson Adams held, was beneath the notice of a philosopher, how much more negligible by a west-country laird—a Boswell or a Craiglands! 'You know my grand object,' says the former, 'is the ancient family of Auchinleck, a venerable and noble principle.' 'Is't not as clear as a pike-staff,' says the latter in *Sir Andrew Wylie*, 'that trade and traffic are to be the ruin of the country?' Weavers in coaches! 'I would as soon sit in a Relief Kirk,' he declares, 'as darken the door o' ony sic cattle.' Galt draws a picture of these gentry in the *Annals*, sulking in their castles, and almost willing to have forgone the rise in value of their lands rather than have witnessed the 'incoming of o'er sea speculation.' They could not be brought to admit (and it is hard to blame them) that the romance had gone out of their tiny feudalism; that it had deserted the castles for the factories. 'A new genius,' says Mr. Balwhidder, 'had descended upon the earth, and there was an erect and outlooking spirit abroad that was not to be satisfied with the taciturn regularity of ancient affairs.' The true romance was in the working of this spirit; and it is still there in spite of politics and congresses. The men of the age, emerging from the waste and disorder of centuries into the steady contentments of prosperity, felt as Pennant the traveller felt when he issued suddenly from the bleak Highland glens of the west upon the opening plains of the Lowlands. 'I was struck with rapture,' he says, 'at a sight so new to me . . . The vale between the end of the lake and Dunbarton is unspeakably beautiful, very fertile, and finely watered by the great and rapid river Levin: there is scarcely a spot on its banks but what is decorated with bleacheries, plantations and villas.' Even Miss Pringle, the fair, the romantic Miss Pringle, did not escape the contagion of the time. As she passed through Ardrossan on the beginning of that memorable journey after the legacy, 'What a monument,' she exclaimed, 'has the late Earl of Eglinton left there of his public spirit! It should embalm his memory in the hearts of future ages, *as I doubt not but in time Ardrossan will become a grand emporium*'! This is the true material sublime. When the women speak like this the pioneer may breathe freely. For the cause is assured.

It is sometimes said that if Galt had written only one novel, as Goldsmith did, he would have been better remembered. It is very probable. But these delicate considerations of posthumous fame are seldom the immediate concern of the author who writes for a living; and when the public mind is the object to be reached, economy may be as dangerous as extravagance. 'Had I only written *Waverley*,' says Walter Scott, 'I should have long since been, according to the established phrase, "the ingenious author of a novel much admired at the time."' Of course Galt wrote too much; and, what is worse, he was constantly deserting his natural inclination and disguising his talent in uncongenial styles. The best of his novels in the high manner, *Sir Andrew Wylie*, was deliberately altered, on the advice of some friends, to suit the current taste; the extravagant and romantic elements of the story were no part of his original plan, which was simply the exhibition of the rise and progress of a humble Scot in London. There is nothing more dangerous to a man who possesses some native and original vein than the advice of friends. After the first display of his powers they set themselves, from mere kindness of heart, to tempt him into the ranks of convention. A needy author is generally in the worst possible position to resist such advances; and Galt succumbed, like Scott, knowing better. It is a melancholy thing to reflect how many tales of Scottish manners we have lost because Ballantyne the printer thought the *Antiquary* low, and 'roared for chivalry,' and because Galt's friends preferred his Lord Sandyfords and Lady Blessingtons to the quieter merits of his more homely characters. He had no grip of manners outside his familiar experience. His high-born young ladies 'bound like fawns amidst the stately groves that surround the venerable magnificence of their ancestral home'; his noblemen talk a language never spoken on earth, which is only appropriate because they act from motives of such ghostly possibility that no other language could express them. There is nothing in his most ambitious compositions to be compared with the death-scene of Mr. Cayenne (one of the most daring things in fiction); nothing so genially humorous as the picture in the *Annals*, when the recruiting party came, of Mr. Balwhidder and Mr. Archibald Dozendale the elder agreeing over a sober tumbler of toddy that the end of the world was drawing nearer and nearer. Galt has been long enough dead, however, to be remembered by his best work and forgotten in his worst. His genuine originality has been obscured by the reputation of contemporaries and by his own depreciation of his writings. But, though he disclaimed all conscious rivalry with Sir Walter Scott, he never forgot that the *Annals* was written a year before the publication of *Waverley*, and that he was 'the senior in Scottish historical sketches.'

It may seem a bold thing to suggest that Galt has been neglected by his own countrymen, who have always prided themselves, above other nations, on loyalty to their own writers. But the fact is beyond denial. The present generation at least knows little or nothing about him. The west of Scotland had the good fortune to produce, at the most important time in its history, both a poet and a chronicler of its manners. Each was of singular merit in his kind, and there was no reason why the genius of the one should ever have oppressed the genuine talent of the other. This, however, is what has happened, through that blind appropriation of Burns by the multitude which has converted the republic of Scottish letters into something approaching an absolute monarchy. Local enthusiasm has been turned into the general channel; Galt is little read, even in the west; and poetry has registered yet another irrelevant triumph over prose.

That to English readers Galt should be much known was not to be expected. They have begun, however, to exhibit a more generous curiosity in the social mysteries of their northern neighbours, and many even profess to have arrived at some proficiency in the dialect. This has become easier since Stevenson, who skilfully whittled it for uses of style. Indeed, in most of the Scottish stories published nowadays, something of the same compromise has been reached as Caledonian singers employ with so much applause in their dialect songs to London audiences. But Galt belonged to an older age, when broad Scots was still talked in law-courts and drawing-rooms; and some of his west-country words have been thought unusual enough to justify a glossary. It should be some comfort to the English amateur to be assured that many of them are as little known to the modern Scot as they are to himself.

THE CHRONICLES OF THE CANONGATE

(1827-1828)

'GOD make this a happy year to the King and country and to all honest men!' So Sir Walter Scott in the thick of his misfortunes, but heartened by his triumphal French tour and the friendliness of London, entered up his Journal on 1st January 1827. He added the next day a resolution 'to mark down no more griefs and groans.' The worst was over, being known; it was a relief, whatever happened, to have done with 1826. If only 'this bitch of a rheumatism' would take vacations and give up nailing him in his only serviceable knee! Still, he would make the best of her; if she made a prisoner of him, his *Life of Napoleon* would get on the faster. The sixth volume of that grinding task was completed early in the year, amidst the distracting humiliations of leeches, poultices, embrocations and flannels. His Journal, as he complains, takes on 'a vile chirurgical aspect,' with R a too frequent symbol, and even RR (or Rheumatism Redoubled) merely because he had dined with Jeffrey the night before. I begin, he notes ruefully, to be 'quite unfit for a good fellow.' He allowed himself, in fact, few such evenings now, and for reasons not merely of health and the publicity of his affairs shrank a little from society. He was keenly, even morbidly conscious of the growing vacuity in the ranks of his early friends, and of the steady narrowing of companionship: 'in age companionship is ended, except rarely, and by appointment.' He was also, for perhaps the first time in his rich and confident life, bullied by his conscience and dominated by his work. His Journal of those days is pathetically full of private hoistings of the standard, of secret monitions of encouragement, of determinations to ask no mercy.

> 'It appears to me that what is least forgiven in a man of any mark or likelihood is want of that blackguardly article called *pluck*. All the fine qualities of genius cannot make amends for it. We are told the genius of poets, especially, is irreconcilable with this species of grenadier accomplishment. If so, *quel chien de genre*!'

It is good to hear such talk from a great writer in distress at a time when authors of all sizes were cheapening literature with their cant of genius, and cheapening life by deserting their women and living on their friends.

We shall never know how deeply Scott felt the forced disclosure of the secret of *Waverley*. His original intention was never to have avowed these works in his lifetime, and the original manuscripts were preserved (though in other hands than his) to supply the necessary evidence when the day of announcement should arrive. It was a grief to him—'an addition, though a small one, to other annoyances'—that in August, 1831, while he was writing his *Waverley* prefaces, a number of these manuscripts were advertised for public sale. There could, of course, be no question of concealment after the ruin of his affairs, and it was a wise manœuvre of his friend Lord Meadowbank to trap him into a personal confession at the first public dinner at which he had appeared since his misfortunes. This was the Theatrical Fund Dinner held in the Edinburgh Assembly Rooms on 23rd February 1827; Scott was in the chair and seems to have taken the incident well. He had not expected, he said, that in coming there he would have the task of acknowledging, before 300 gentlemen, a secret which, considering that it was communicated to more than twenty people, had been remarkably well kept. He was now before the bar of his country. Into the reasons of his long silence he thought it unnecessary to enter; perhaps caprice might have had a considerable share in it. He now, however, acknowledged his authorship, and when he said that he was the author of those works, he meant seriously to state that he was the total and undivided author. This, evidently, still needed saying, and he was careful to repeat it, later in the year, in his signed preface to the First Series of the *Chronicles of the Canongate*. The last mist of conjecture was blown away. The *Edinburgh Weekly Journal*, quick to grasp the more than provincial importance of these announcements, was rewarded by reproduction in every European newspaper.

Reading its report to-day, one is struck by the Dick Swivellerish air of the dinner, with its glees and sentiments and florid superloyal toasts. Scott is 'the worthy Baronet,' and, when he retires from the chair, does so 'amidst long, loud and rapturous cheering.' As the evening advanced one chairman succeeded another, and the banquet ended with a 'few choice spirits' gathered round a Captain Broadhead of the 7th Hussars; at what hour they broke up we are not specifically told. Two bands exhilarated the proceedings; and 'it is but justice to Mr. Gibb to state,' says the Journal parochially, 'that the dinner was very handsome (though slowly served in) and the wines good.'

Scott's decision to break the series of his Tales and start the *Chronicles of the Canongate*, though taken earlier on other grounds, was no doubt hastened by these events. His mask, he confessed, like my Aunt Dinah's in *Tristram Shandy*, had begun to wear a little thin. He now designed to relax a little from the discipline of three-decker romance, and conduct in the *Chronicles* a narrative miscellany. It was much easier to write tales like 'The Highland Widow' and 'The Three Drovers' than another *Waverley*, and till Boney was safely penned 'in the knotty entrails of St. Helena' he had neither time nor strength for more. They were mostly written when his *Napoleon* had got ahead of the printers, or when he felt the want of the only rest he could allow himself, a change of labour. Lockhart notes at this time a serious alteration in Scott's habits. Formerly, however great the amount of work he put through his hands, his evenings were reserved for the light reading of an elbow-chair or the society of his family and friends. Now he seemed to grudge every minute not spent at the desk. He still rose before six, but now worked night and day—'serving double tides,' 'working tightly,' 'feaguing it away.' Everything in his old habits was looked into, as by a man gravely entering on a new and testing experience. He gave up smoking for a time, thinking that he might be 'less muzzy after dinner': 'at any rate, it breaks a custom—I despise custom.' And always he stands on guard against day-dreams and self-pity. His day-dreams were over, though he could 'see as many castles in the clouds as any man, as many genii in the curling smoke of a steam-engine.' His life had been spent in day-dreams: was he not paying for them now? He tested his bodily strength, feeling about for the old vigour, and sometimes for a moment half persuaded himself it might be there. 'Home covered with snow. . . . I am not sorry to find I can stand a brush of weather yet.' At Abbotsford, well knowing that Tom Purdie would have kept him to the sheltered ground, he slipped out to try himself in a gale, and was encouraged and consoled by having faced it.

> 'There's a touch of the old spirit in me yet, that bids me brave the tempest—the spirit that, in spite of manifold infirmities, made me a roaring boy in my youth, a desperate climber, a bold rider, a deep drinker, and a stout player at single-stick, of all which valuable qualities there are now but slender remains.'

It was on this topic (because he needed strength so much) that he found it hardest to be restrained; time and again he breaks his rule, as some impotence strikes him, and stretches out to his lost youth and health. Old memories rise up, and unman him; friends die, and he is shaken with a fierce contempt for the frailty and littleness of human life.

> 'O God! what are we? Lords of Nature? Why, a tile drops from a housetop, which an elephant would not feel more than the fall of a sheet of pasteboard, and there lies his lordship. Or something of inconceivably minute origin—the pressure of a bone or the inflammation of a particle of the brain—takes place, and the emblem of the Deity destroys himself or someone else. We hold our health and our reason on terms slighter

than one would desire, were it in their choice, to hold an Irish cabin.'

This is not the Scott we know, or that he allowed the world to know; but there is a Hamlet, no doubt of it, in us all.

Boney was finished off on a June morning in 1827, and Scott turned once more 'a blue eye' on his affairs. With these nine volumes behind him, and orders pouring in, he could afford to forget that the Leith Bank had been rude to him about an overdraft of £8, and that Abud the Jew, a dissident and shifty creditor, had nearly driven him to the Canongate Sanctuary. The Highland tales of his Canongate Chronicle (just how appositely named?) were taken up again with vigour, and to fill the day he even started on a boy's History of Scotland. The *Tales of a Grandfather*, which was to sell better than anything since *Ivanhoe*, alternates in his Journal with the lucubrations of Mr. Chrystal Croftangry. It is characteristic of Scott that even now, with his secret out, he could not dispense with a mask, or with the habit of an imaginary coadjutor. Chrystal succeeds Jedediah, and, what is remarkable, beats him hollow at the part. Scott has done nothing better of their kind than the Croftangry Introductions to the two series of the Chronicles, and it is a pity they are so seldom read. Chrystal in many ways is Scott himself, and we may still catch in these neglected pages some of the hidden or half-hidden history of his life and family: traits of his mother in Mrs. Bethune Baliol, of the Scotts of Raeburn in the Croftangrys of Castle Treddles, and of his ever-consistent father in Mr. Fairscribe. This last is to the life, and rivals the portrait in *Redgauntlet*. The public, unfortunately, was not ripe for this bounty, or not sufficiently in the secret of it, and the stories, on the whole, were of an inferior cast. As the copy came in there was a good deal of the old nagging from James Ballantyne, who had never liked the Canongate plan, and objected even to 'The Two Drovers,' which of the three stories in that consignment is incomparably the best. Scott took unusual trouble to meet James's criticisms (and his own misgivings), even cancelling two sheets, though he disliked re-writing as much as Falstaff hated paying back. 'The Drovers' must not be touched. 'The Highland Widow,' on the other hand, though the old skill is there and the old cunning play of contrasts, was never, perhaps, alive; and 'The Surgeon's Daughter,' after a good beginning in a Scottish village, is smothered in melodrama and curry-powder. It is his own word for the local colour somewhat hastily acquired from an Anglo-Indian colonel who came over to breakfast for the purpose.

The work was finished in September, 1827—on a Sunday, too, 'God forgive me'—and had the cool reception which J.B. had so annoyingly predicted. Even Cadell, Scott's new publisher, was worried, and there was a consultation and a weighing of forces. Scott put it to them both that the time had probably come when he must lie fallow as a novelist, but they refused to listen and he consented to try again. Their appeals and remonstrances seem to-day, and to a reader of the Journal, a kind of cruelty, but their persistence was rewarded. After one or two false starts—*My Aunt Margaret's Mirror* and *The Laird's Jock*, which neither Ballantyne nor Cadell would accept—he fell plump into the vein of *The Fair Maid of Perth*. It was like old times; and perhaps from that day to this no story of Scott's has given more genuine pleasure. Though not, as Lockhart says, among his performances 'of the first file,' it is a work brilliantly designed, and has scenes, though not characters, equal to his best. Ballantyne was happy to watch the Canongate Miscellany burst asunder, and the Author of *Waverley* emerge.

Scott worked at *The Fair Maid* (and at his *Tales of a Grandfather*) through the winter of 1827 and the early spring of 1828, eyed critically, as usual, by his printer. On 21st February he stuck—'watching and waiting till I hit on some quaint and clever mode of extricating.' What was this? How to deal with Ramorny's potentialities, and make his villainy stage-manage the last scenes? Whatever the knot he untied it, and, 'the blackdog' and *hysterica passio* notwithstanding, the story went on. To the character of Conachar he gave a care and attention which, but for Lockhart's elucidation, could not have been properly understood. He had in mind, as he wrote, the unhappy fate of his brother Daniel, and how he had declined to attend his funeral or wear mourning for him. The philosophy of courage and cowardice he now recognized as one of the obscurest fields of human speculation:

'My secret motive, in this attempt [he said], was to perform a sort of expiation to my poor brother's *manes*. I have now learned to have more tolerance and compassion than I had in those days.'

Ballantyne, though he rubbed his hands over *The Maid*, as the sheets arrived was prolific of criticism. Was the time-table right? Was it, for example, quite late enough for the glee-girl to be thinking of a night's rest? And must the Bonnet-maker die? Could not his creator spare him? Scott's answer to all this is so massively patient and so wise in grain that it must be cited. The question of time was easily dispatched—'I counted the hours with accuracy'—and the poor girl was brought within an hour of sunset. As to the Bonnet-maker, and the plea for mercy:

'I cannot afford to be merciful to Master Oliver Proudfute, although I am heartily glad there is any one of the personages sufficiently interesting to make you care whether he lives or dies. But it would cost my cancelling half a volume, and rather than do so, I would, like the valiant Baron of Clackmannan, kill the whole characters, the author, and the printer. Besides, *entre nous*, the resurrection of Athelstane was a botch. It struck me when I was reading *Ivanhoe* over the other day.'

So much for *The Maid*. As to criticism generally, 'I value yours,' says Scott, 'as much as ever':

'but the worst is, my faults are better known to myself than to you. Tell a young beauty that she wears an unbecoming dress, or an ill-fashioned ornament, or speaks too loud, or commits any other mistake which she can correct, and she will do so, if she has sense, and a good opinion of your taste. But tell a fading beauty that her hair is getting grey, her wrinkles apparent, her gait heavy, and that she has no business in a ballroom but to be ranged against the wall as an evergreen, and you will afflict the poor old lady, without rendering her any service. She knows all that better than you.'

In one country, at any rate, and in the most illustrious circle of that country, there was none of this criticism. Goethe, a year before, had exchanged greetings with Sir Walter, a salute of aged or ageing giants. Scott had a rule seldom to read, and never to answer letters from foreign admirers; the thing was meaningless and endless. 'But Goethe is different and a wonderful fellow.' He had always been one of Scott's most loyal adherents, and it was a family joke that when he opened a new *Waverley*, there was no speaking to him till he had finished the third volume: 'He was worse than any girl at a boarding-school with her first novel!' He had now, this year, read *The Fair Maid of Perth*, and, when Eckermann began it in the autumn of 1828, took a pleasure in discussing it with him. 'Isn't it good?' he began. 'There's a real bit of work! There's a master-hand! The design so sure, and in the details not a stroke that does not lead to the goal. And what detail! The dialogue and descriptive setting all equally excellent . . . How far have you got?' 'I've come to the place,' said Eckermann, 'where Henry Smith leads the pretty zither-girl through streets and byways home, and where to his annoyance the bonnet-maker Proutfut and the apothecary Dwining meet him.' 'Yes,' said Goethe, 'it's a good place. That the reluctant honest armourer should be brought so far as to carry the questionable maiden's luggage, and at last the dog too, is one of the greatest strokes in any novel; it points to a knowledge and insight into the deepest secrets of human nature.' 'I must also admire,' said Eckermann, 'his making the father of the heroine a glover, who has long been in truck with the Highlanders through his trade in skins and hides, and is still.' 'Yes,' said Goethe, who saw very well the quiet adroitness of a *liaison* which gave Conachar a home in Perth. But there was, indeed, no limit to his admiration: 'the King, the Royal brother, the Crown Prince, the Prior, the noblemen, the magistrate, the burghers and artisans—all drawn with equal sureness and caught with equal truth.' 'The

English,' said Frau von Goethe, for she had come in and sat down, 'are particularly fond of the character of Henry Smith, and Walter Scott also seems to have made him the hero of the book. He is not my favourite. I prefer the Prince.' 'Ah,' said Goethe, after some further conversation, 'you women are wrong when you always take a side. You generally read a book to find nourishment for your heart, a hero whom you might love. But that's not really how one should read. The question isn't at all whether that character or this should please you, but whether the book should please you.' 'But we women are like that, dear father,' said Frau von Goethe, nodding and pressing his hand. 'Well, it doesn't matter,' said Goethe. 'One must indulge you in your ways.'

The discussion was renewed a few days later, Goethe's interest as keen as ever, and one scene after another was taken up. Eckermann read English slowly, but Goethe encouraged him to go on.

> 'And when you have finished with *The Fair Maid of Perth*, you must immediately read *Waverley*, which still looks out with quite different eyes, and unquestionably is to be placed beside the best things that have ever been written in the world. One sees it is the same man who has done *The Fair Maid of Perth*, but a man who had first of all to win the favour of the public and brace himself to produce nothing short of excellence. *The Fair Maid of Perth*, on the other hand, is written with a broader pen. The author is by this time sure of his public, and lets himself go a bit more freely. When one has read *Waverley*, one understands well why Walter Scott still calls himself always the author of that work, for he showed there what he could do, and he has never written anything since that was better or even equal to that first novel.'

Few authors enjoy hearing, after a lifetime of labour, that their first work was their best, but Scott would not have minded. It would have warmed him to the heart to know that in Weimar, in the year 1828, such things were being said, and that Goethe could be so happy discussing a work of his decline. The advice which Goethe gave to Eckermann, when he had finished with *The Maid* to go back to *Waverley*, still stands.

147

ANDREW LANG

IT is a melancholy thing to be presented one day with a new and delightful book and to be informed on the next that its author is dead. Andrew Lang died a day or two after this book [1] appeared, before the public had had time to do more than turn its pages and admire the versatility of a writer to whom nothing that was humane was ever difficult. So much youth, one would have thought, must have resisted death a little longer, for he had the spirit of play, and all his books were adventures; but, as he might himself have said with Cromwell, he had 'done his do.' There is a gravity in the last sentence of his preface beyond the immediate purpose; and it is probable that he felt, what none of his readers will feel, the weight of those 664 pages. 'That sins of commission as well as of omission will be discovered the author cannot doubt, for through much reading and writing they that look out of window are darkened.' Few men of his generation can have read more or written more than he, or defied darkness so long. There is only one consolation in his death, that no man had more questions to ask of the next world. His Gowrie Conspiracies and Casket Letters, his sunken galleons, his ghosts and tribes, his men in greatcoats with the gun in their hand, now puzzle him no more, nor his real Homer. One stroke of death has solved all his mysteries, and in solving them has silenced as much humour and humanity as the world of letters could point to in one man.

It is sometimes said, when a man of many attachments dies, that he had an instinct for friendship. Lang had something as rare, something higher and drier, an instinct for fraternity. He was before all things a brother of the craft. The angler and the archaeologist, the historian and the poet, the scholar and the journalist, the spiritualist and anthropologist—he was at

---

[1] *History of English Literature from 'Beowulf' to Swinburne.*

home among them all, a member of their guild. Like his master Scott, he dearly loved a man of his hands—a man who could *do* something. He was in his generation the ambassador of all the sporting crafts at the court of letters, and in his own master-craft of book-making (for no man knew better the force of the maxim, *c'est un métier de faire un livre*) had no equal out of France. He was, indeed, both for his reading and writing the greatest bookman of our age, and after Stevenson the best man of letters of the Scottish tradition in the last half century. It is to be hoped that Scotland will honour his memory, for no man understood or loved her better, exile though he was, having accepted his domicile, and whose cause was in the past. His charming English, even, is the English of an *émigré*. It has the nicety of a foreigner, like Stevenson's, or like Anthony Hamilton's French. It has what Englishmen call 'something Gallic' in it; for by an instinct which history may explain, Scots writers have always gone more to the Latin than to the English tradition for their last lessons in style. Lang was in the old Scots tradition. Had Edinburgh remained what it was in Scott's time, he might have been a second Scott. In these latter days, when wits no longer think it necessary to be scholars, his merits had begun to look old-fashioned. Such a range of the humanities seemed old-world to the young. There was the mark of the vintage on them. He had, besides, the old instinct of the man of letters for the avoidance of politics, and nowadays all our flourishing young writers are politicians first and men of letters by accident. Lang left these things to the men of Edinburgh with their law and their logic. His chance of politics went out with the Stuarts and the Calamity of Culloden.

That such a man should write a good text-book is as natural as that good text-books should be rare, for to write such a thing a man must know himself even better than his subject. A great part of the singular merit of the *History of English Literature* is its truth to its author, so that from this book alone you might write a history of Lang. He begins a little reluctantly—the Anglo-Saxon poems are 'those very old poems'—but it is wonderful how he brightens up when he gets to the historians, to biography, and things. William of Malmesbury and Gerald the Welshman rise up in his hands, and Gerald's *Little Tour of Ireland* may yet find readers among the readers of Lang. Where other historians are dullest he is often at his best. Wearied by the *enjambement* school of critics and the analyses of form which fill our histories of literature, with what refreshment we come upon a man whose first inclination is not to scan his author but to hear what he says! Poor shuffling Occleve, the stock example of fifteenth-century dullness, surprises us in this book by becoming a human being, an amateur Villon without genius; and Ascham, the schoolmaster, turns out something of a dicer and cock-fighter, to his advantage. Not that Lang is neglectful of form. He even detects Macaulay in a sentence of William of Malmesbury about the First Crusade: 'The Welshman left his hunting, the Scot his fellowship with lice, the Dane his drinking party, the Norwegian his raw fish.' It is the very authentic big drum. With this love of things goes his love of stories. The historians of literature never relate them, though they are at the heart of literature. It is possible that they assume them; it is more probable that they do not know them. Lang is never content with what are called 'appreciations.' When he speaks of the Romances (and he speaks of them with relish) his first idea is not to hunt them down, but to say what they are about. When he talks of King Horn, he gives the story of King Horn; how Rymenhild fainted—'one of the earliest faints executed by any heroine in English fiction.' When he describes the making of the mediaeval Tale of Troy he does not merely say that it was 'gradually transformed by various accretions and the characters defined'; he says that Cassandra, in the end, 'gleyit a little, had a slight cast of the eye, like Mary Stuart.' If the attention of youth were more often addressed, as Lang addresses it, to the body of literature, they would be less likely to miss its soul. But what is to be hoped from a critical tradition which has ceased to remember that literature is about things?

It is part of Lang's habit of mind that he considers the modern reader, who probably does not wish to read very bad verse because it preceded better. He divides poets into two classes, those who may be read with pleasure, and those who must be written about, and is careful to make it plain to which class, in his opinion, our several poets belong. This is good sense, and his opinion on such a matter is obviously of the first value. The cult of the dead minor has gone so far that future ages may be puzzled to distinguish which poets we liked and which poets we merely wrote about for preferment or hire. This unprofessional detachment gives Lang a great strength. Undeceived by the historical attitude to the Jacobean poets he can see just how low they are in the scale of greatness and how greatness comes in.

'These poets,' he says, 'are not now commonly read, except in selections of their best things, and such selections give no idea of their pervading faults. When we extend our knowledge of the authors, and mark the formless character of the age in poetry, the sudden appearance of Milton indicates as great a miracle of genius as the existence of Chaucer, Spenser and Shakespeare in the throng of their contemporaries.'

Such judgments become almost impossible for the historical student who has probably forgotten, in the chaos of 'origin' and 'influence,' what it is to read a book for itself and to judge it directly like a man. That other fallacy of the parasites of literature, which represents it as a sacred profession and its greater practitioners as saints and martyrs, receives no countenance from Lang. Life was too strong. Langland 'must have been, in some ways, not unlike Mr. Thomas Carlyle. Though he has a noble appreciation of the dignity and duty of manual labour—the honest and pious ploughman was his favourite character—he never did toil with his hands.' As for Hooker, the favourite example of the good author in difficulties, he took a living in Buckinghamshire, says Lang demurely, and 'experienced "the corroding cares that attend a married priest." Among these was reading Horace while he watched his sheep, and rocking his child's cradle.' *His* child's, observe, and we are out of sentiment into life. The more modern and less creditable affectation which has made the lives of our poets of the early nineteenth century turn on a sickly record of first love affairs finds Lang at one with Peacock and common sense. 'Much more has been made of both these affairs than they are worth,' says Peacock, speaking of Shelley's Miss Grove and Byron's Miss Chaworth. 'It is probable that few of Johnson's poets passed through their boyhood without a similar attachment, but if it came at all under the notice of our literary Hercules, he did not think it worth recording.' Will not someone follow his example? The literary history of the Romantic Revival will never be sane until we learn to understand, with Johnson, and ignore.

To the older generation which has been reading Lang these thirty years, this book will be most interesting, as it reveals, in a hundred odd corners and crannies of speech, the private and domestic mind of its author. And to begin with, what a dominie he would have made, in some better Gander-cleugh! Even from a dying man he will exact his quantities. 'Carried away by grief when his wife murders his surviving boy, Gorboduc pronounces the name of Eubulus with the penultimate syllable short, and expires with decency behind the scenes.' He will concede, with the instructed generosity of an old hand, the splendour and audacity of Pope's *Iliad*, but as for his essay on pastorals—'it would have been pleasant to set down Pope to the construing of a few passages from Theocritus.' He likes to know what a boy *did* at school —if he played for it and so on. Byron, despite his lameness, played for Harrow against Eton, and 'by a strange coincidence the printed score of the match (the manuscript was burned in a fire at Lord's) docks Byron of half his runs, and apparently confers them on Mr. Shakespeare!' Byron, he adds, 'was a change-bowler.' His familiar interest in witches and spectres seems to have dated from childhood. When he relates Lamb's childish awe of the picture in Stackhouse— 'the Witch Raising of Samuel, which I wish I had never seen'—it is to tell us that his own childhood was 'dominated' by the same picture. He could never resist a ghost. The other virtues of Richard Baxter, numerous as they were, might scarcely have obtained him a place in this survey had he not 'loved a good ghost story' and 'left on record an excellent death-wraith'; nor can the author conceal from us that he thinks quite appreciably better of Addison because 'like Coleridge in talk with Keats, he deals in ghost stories,' and in an age of reason 'does not scout them.' It is no small part of his interest in Defoe that his favourite topic was 'psychical research' or of his interest in ghosts that Sir Walter Scott was also a ghost-hunter. For Sir Walter is his guiding star, his hero of letters. The ties of race, which bind every Scot to Sir Walter, in Lang were filial. He was his great exemplar; and when he seeks for a literary parallel or a crowning judgment he turns first, as by right of instinct, to the life or writings of Scott. What are we to say of his other enthusiasms, for his native borders and their streams, for the Jacobites and Mary Stuart, for Joan of Arc? The year when the Maid was burned, the year when Mary was beheaded, were crucial dates to him in the moral chronology of England. When he mentions Warwick it is to add that he was the cruel gaoler of the Maid at Rouen, or the *Cenci*, that the heroine was more cruelly treated even than she; nor can John Fletcher, the dramatist, get himself properly born without all the world knowing that his father was 'that Dean of Peterborough who troubled the last moments of Mary.' Lang could not forget these things, and when he comes to Burke and his fine sentence about 'chivalry'—'When,' he cries, 'was there an age of chivalry? If no swords leaped from their sheaths for Marie Antoinette in 1793, not one was drawn for Jeanne d'Arc in 1431, not one for Mary Stuart in 1587.' As for Froude, how contrive to be patient with a historian so ignorant of all things Scottish as to be 'wedded to the belief that James I was the first of the Stuart line'? It was always James VI and I to Lang, and, if occasion demanded, James VIII and III. Young, the poet, comes along with some trumped-up adulation of the Duke of Newcastle in 1745, when

A Pope-bred princeling crawled ashore:

meaning, says Lang:

> The Prince who did in Moidart land
> With seven men on his right hand
> And all to conquer kingdoms three
> Oh, he's the lad to wanton me!

Is it not glorious, after forty years at the desk, to feel like this: to flush at a name, and be a boy again at the magic of a date and an old song? When we are told, in the pages on Fielding, that Prince Charlie, then lurking in a Parisian convent, purchased *Tom Jones* both in French and English, or that the footman who attended Sterne on his death-bed was 'a Macdonald of the Keppoch branch, whose father was out in the Forty-five,' let us not be so insensible as to imagine that we are listening merely to the curiosities of an historian. We are doing much more than that. We are assisting at the perpetual obsequies of romance.

One more Cause, and I have done. Lang was a Borderer, and therefore an angler, a lover of streams. After Scott there is, perhaps, no name which occurs more frequently in these pages than the name of Izaak Walton—'a mere fisher with bait,' it is true, but for the beauty of his style and the sweetness of his thought worthy of lavender. The remarks on the cruelty of angling in Donne's 'Bait' Lang thought must have 'hurt Izaak to the heart' when he was writing the Dean's life. His favourite streams, though he loves a good stream anywhere, are the streams of the Border, and, above all, 'the glittering and resolute streams of Tweed.' If only Drayton had not stopped at the Cumberland Eden, with all the Scottish rivers before him from the Debatable Land to the Naver! Yet he praises the *Polyolbion* and recommends it to anglers for 'the minute knowledge which its author has of even such burns as the "roaring Yarty" . . . and the troutful Minram.' Had Drayton said more about his streams and been less earnest

> the battle in to bring

he thinks, with justice, that the poem would have had more

attractions. Once more we see his love of things, of the 'object.' When he finds a poet, like Gay, setting up to write on *Rural Sports*, he does not dismiss his efforts in the usual formula as 'an example of the growing interest in Nature.' He is interested in what Gay may have to say, and, looking to see what truth there is in Gay, he tries him by angling:

'Gay's descriptions of Nature, and his praises, are more genuine than, in that age of the Town, such things usually were. He writes of angling "with his eye on the object" . . . His remarks on fishing with the worm, a theme unworthy of the Muse, are judicious. As to fly-fishing, Gay is among those who advocate a search for the insect in the waters and an exact imitation. He would have us fish "fine and far off," with "a single hair" next the hook, and perhaps he is the first to recommend the use of the "dry" or floating fly— "Upon the curling *surface* let it glide," not sunk . . . For his own part, he never uses either worm or the natural fly: never tries for coarse fish—pike, perch, and so forth—and this justifies the affection of his friends.' How excellent and health-giving for the clever young men who despise everything beneath the rank of a general idea, and think that literature is something about style!

WALTER RALEIGH

'What's he, the tall fellow?'
'You may say the great one.
There's not his like in Oxford, a full scholar. . . .
—Sir, if I were a painter, I would draw him
Standing colossally above his fellows;
Give him a book (which since it should contain
The learning that you cannot find in books)
Should be no smaller than a galleon's sail,
Lend him, for a desk to read from, Magdalen tower.
Then would you see him shake the pinnacles.
While from the ground the murmuring schools applauded
The echo of his wit.—But come, to dinner!
And after dinner you shall praise the city.'
                                        —'The Cloisterers.'

THE death of Walter Raleigh, in the full grandeur of his
powers, has impoverished the two generations of his friends.
So much wisdom and gaiety, such noble perceptions, such
unconquerable youth, seemed made for some longer con-
tinuance, and to the least imaginative of his acquaintance
suggested some human foretaste of immortality. It was an
endowment to life that he should be alive. These were kindly
illusions at which he would have been the first to smile. He
held his existence on another tenure, knowing well, like all
true poets and adventurers, that the price of life is danger,
and life at best but 'a losing match nobly played.' He played
his last set like a boy. It had been an agony to him that in the
great trial of England he could not take a soldier's part. The
long arm of the war touched him on the shoulder after all;
and he died, not of rust and disuse, but of action and adventure, as nearly as possible the death he wished. His friends
have lost an incomparable companion, and England one of
her best and most understanding lovers.

He is principally known as a literary critic; but his study

156

was life, and his profession was living. Of literary criticism, in
which he excelled, he had no time a very high opinion. He
was well aware that on its greatest themes, so far as this art is
judicial, it is in the end not the author but the critic who is
judged. His standard of criticism was lofty; he considered it
a trade of 'disheartening difficulty.' In the later ease of his
maturity he valued it less for its duties than for the opportunities: as the discourse unrolled, he would pay himself,
from time to time, with marginalia on the world. These are
the richest parts of his writings, and will live.

His best known books are probably his *Style* and his
Shakespeare. The first he wrote when he was a young professor, as a holiday reward for having achieved a text-book,
his still highly marketable 'English Novel.' He was not proud
of *Style*, though its sale amused him; it was his carnival of
rhetoric, and the last. He called it a 'conceited book,' 'dandy-
ish,' and 'clever,' and asked that the wilfulness of youth should
be forgiven. Of cleverness he was no great admirer, even in
the young: preferring, sometimes, a puzzled sincerity. The
wits of the last age, the dynasty of Chestertons, who fell in
love with cleverness, he found 'not helpful.' As for style, he
came to believe that the secret of it is only frankness and
sincerity: to tell the truth if one can. He was himself, in all
the uses of expression, a frugal master, scorning the spend-
thrift success he might so easily have had. *Style*, then, was
outlived. It is, nevertheless, a book which few young men
could have written, and which not many seniors, had they
written it, could afford to discard. It has had one bad effect,
of early misrepresenting its author's character. It is, as he
somewhere complains, the eternal habit of the public, when
it meets with anything new, to be unhappy until it has
named it, and when it has named it, to be for ever at rest.
Walter Raleigh was hailed on the strength of this book as a
wit and the Mercutio of professors; and ever since, when the
two essences have seemed to be disengageable, his readers
have taken his wit and left his wisdom. It could not be supposed that an author was wholly in earnest who was never
dull. Even his *Shakespeare*, though a work of his maturity

and an acknowledged masterpiece of its kind, is probably best known to his older readers for its trouncing of the 'entomologists of criticism' and its dismissal of Shakespeare's biographers as the compilers of 'a scrap-heap of respectable size.' Younger readers are righting this balance, and begin to be aware, by certain signs, that since Charles Lamb no critic has appeared so perfectly equipped for the Shakespearian task in the first requisite of human experience and knowledge of the heart of man. At the romantic auction of Shakespearian praise he set the example, now more popular, of keeping one's head in the presence of genius, and suggested that insensibility may not be the right word for a determination to regard Shakespeare as an English rather than as a world poet and to review his work rationally and historically as a whole. More than any other man he is responsible for the revival in public esteem of the 'cool and manly utterances' of Dryden and Johnson, and for the resuscitation of Morgann's forgotten masterpiece. Shakespeare has had few readers like Walter Raleigh and, when he warms to his task, no better critic. His book will yield, in time, like all criticism, to traditional selection; and the great passages of the first and fifth chapters, in which the mind of Shakespeare is shown at work, will take their place by the side of Johnson's 'Preface' and the best elucidations of Coleridge, Hazlitt and Lamb.

It has been remarked as singular that his earlier full-drawn studies were of Milton and Wordsworth, of all English poets the most exacting to a critic, and, it might have been thought, the least congenial to Raleigh. The observation is not unnatural, but does less than justice to the seriousness of a critic who on one, at any rate, of these poets has written the best book yet known. It was precisely because of their difficulty, because they were lonely and very great and exacting, that this lover of the valley chose to climb their slopes. It is an unusual spectacle; the penance of Biron, self-imposed. The brilliant young critic goes into retreat, and emerges an expert in the discipline of his craft. He is henceforth enrolled in that 'curious minority' who conceive it to be their duty, in studying a poet, to follow him with patience step by step, through his failures and his triumphs, recreating his experience, hanging on his words, believing in him and living with him. It is a minority of which most of the members are simple folk, and few men of letters are to be found in it. That Raleigh, with talents equal to so much easier and so much more clamorous successes, should voluntarily have entered this community of patience, is a striking testimony to the sincerity of his genius—or, since the word is hackneyed, to his love of truth. It was undoubtedly a strain. There are signs in his 'Milton' that the discipline was severe and was felt to be severe; and now and then, discarding his tools, he will indulge himself on those solemn battlements with unlicensed song and dance. In the later 'Wordsworth' nothing of this appears; the rule has been embraced; and the book remains a masterpiece, without followers or predecessors.

From these altitudes it was a relief to descend and rub shoulders once more with the kindly traffickers of the vale. His taste was for the men who had shaken hands with the world: for Chaucer, Boccaccio, Cervantes, and his Elizabethans, or those later veterans of life, Samuel Johnson and Charles Lamb. He had a great love for mortal man. This loving, striving, sinful world was very dear to him. There is no evidence that our friend deplored the Fall, or was otherwise than reasonably contented with the devices 'introduced by the necessities of sin.' 'The Serpent is glad to escape from Hell to breathe the morning air of Eden; but how glad we are to escape from Eden!' The felicities of Milton's Paradise —roadless, hearthless, and childless—seemed terrifying to this critic. He could not settle down in this 'enormous bliss.' Milton's Hell is more interesting than his Paradise, because it has more and better company; the downy contours of Adam are dull after the scars of Satan. There are so few lines on the faces of our First Parents, and so many on the faces of their enemies. No student of Milton has more grandly described the magnificences of his great poem; but through all its splendours and primordial debates his ear is still listening for another voice. Through the vast spaces of this strange, majestic commonwealth of angels and men, with its shapes passing, its high language and great wars, golden processions moving across the Chaos, and worlds blown and broken like bubbles—in the midst of this gigantic rivalry of systems he hears a cry

> like that muffled cry which caught Macbeth's ear as he nerved himself for his last fight. It is the cry of the human soul, left homeless and derelict in a universe where she is the only alien. For her the amaranth of the empyreal Heaven is as comfortless as the adamant of Hell. She has lost her Paradise even while Adam's was building—the Paradise where the flowers fade, and loves and hates are mortal.

Of this mortal Paradise no more delighted inhabitant can be imagined than Walter Raleigh. He had the secret of all whole-hearted pleasure, never to be afraid of it; and believed, indeed, that the love of pleasure, if only it be generous and sensitive, is hardly to be distinguished from wisdom and tact. No one who is not capable of great happiness (and he has Wordsworth to support him) could, he supposed, be a highly moral being. 'That profanity which is called disillusionment' never touched him. He believed that it could touch no one who had ever been truly happy. He had few illusions. He never flattered himself that life was easy because it was pleasant, or heroic because it was hard. Though his heart was always with the dear and companionable beauty of the world, he knew that the ground on which the graces must build is the beauty of the rocks; that flowers, and laughter, and fragrance are 'the offspring of the same unalterable law which disciplines the stars.' Beneath his gayest talk and wittiest writing there ran always on undertone of tenderness and gravity.

He could forgive almost everything except cruelty, bilking, and the neglect of life. For this last disorder his eye was unerring. He was quick to recognize and to discard the writer who had no claim upon his facts, or no more ownership in them than is conferred by a five minutes' passage from the note-book to the printed page. 'No man can hope to make much impression on a reader with facts which he has not thought it worth his own while to remember.' 'The measure of an author's power,' he declared, 'would be best found in the book which he should sit down to write the day after his library was burnt to the ground.' All his own books are rich in statements which have their warrant from life : in wise and happy sayings, the harvest of sensibility and experience. His most sudden felicities will always bear examination, and be found to have their roots in the business of men. No code of criticism can be extracted from his writings; he followed none and bequeathed none. But—

> There will always remain a certain curious minority of the human race whose desire is not so much to judge a poet as to understand him;
> A criticism of a poet that omits all reference to his failures is as futile a thing as a biography of a great soldier that passes in silence over his defeats;
> We cannot begin to read poetry where our fathers left off; we must begin where they began;
> It is the everlasting difficulty of Shakespeare criticism that the critics are so much more moral than Shakespeare, and so much less experienced;

These and a hundred others are the aphorisms of a master of his craft, and there is no reader or critic so well grounded and accomplished that he can fail to learn from them. In the wider areas of human chance and human conduct, when his subject stops him, he will never be found to refuse a challenge. Some of his briefer sentences on the variorum of life carry still about them the excitement of talk. 'What is failure, in a world where men are mortal?' 'Greatness never comes up in watched places.' 'Every book that can be called a book has had one interested and excited reader.' 'All that is heroic in literature is simple and straightforward, but then, the hero is prepared to die.' 'When a man is ready and willing to sacrifice his life, you cannot deny him the right to choose what he will die for.' 'Most men would forgo their claims to justice for the chance of being liked.' If these sentences be merely wit, what, then, is wisdom?

The mind which expressed itself in this manner was plainly

THE LIVES OF AUTHORS

not stall-fed. In his later years, indeed, he was no great reader. He was of the school of Hobbes: 'if he had read as much as other men he should have known as little.' In his youth he had read eagerly and widely, but when the prime thirst was over he disciplined his taste. The dropsical thirst for books, so often to be found among men cast daily into libraries, he avoided easily. Life was too tempting, and his standard of reading was too high. If the craving returned, he met it like a soldier on the march, and sucked more vigorously the pebble of life. When he read he read whole-heartedly, giving his mind to the business, and his reading partook of the excitement of dialogue. When he turned to literature it was for sustenance; he used it, not like wedding-cake, to dream on, but like bread, to eat. Reading, on this view, could not possibly be incessant, for the work is too hard.

There are people who relax themselves over a book, but this was seldom his way. When he wished for relaxation he took it in talk. An open playground for exuberant activity he believed to be of the first importance for a writer. 'The human mind is playful, and will not be denied its sport.' Even Milton, he would point out, took his holiday, emptying the sluices of his mind in torrential prose. Raleigh, like Johnson, found his playground in talk. Of those delights of the mind which were partaken in his company no description can be given which will not seem idle to his friends and uninstructive to others. In his public writings his pace is ordered; in talk he hunted his topic Shakespearianly, 'with a full cry of hounds.' It was a carnival of fancy, but it was observable that at its wildest this fancy still played with life. He was a master of colloquy. The dealers in smart sayings, the terrible possessors of 'funds of anecdote,' found neither encouragement nor comfort in rooms which, by his merely entering them, became instantly, by some miracle, his club. Monologue fled from him; the word must be tossed and caught; and at every volley the idea must still mount and the phrase be bettered. Life seemed more valuable in his company, and every man to be more himself: it was felt that here or nowhere, now or never, the contagion of life was to be caught.

'He was always the centre of his circle; where he was, there was society.' He could not be unaware that on this most sociable violin of the human voice he fiddled divinely; but his talk was unaffected. It was the delight and glory of his conversation that it was always free, and was born and died with the occasion.

He had an admirable simplicity, and abhorred that pointing of distinctions which is indicated by the ritual of approach. The modern idolatry of genius and 'distinguished talent' seemed to him a vulgar taste, and he did not incline to like a man who submitted to it. 'We must protect ourselves against our great men.' He believed that the elements of genius are less peculiar and less partially distributed than is supposed; that the stuff of genius is the common stuff of humanity somewhat unusually compounded; and that 'no man wholly destitute of genius could live a day.' Poets he believed to be in reality what Wordsworth called them, 'men speaking to men,' and, when they differed from their neighbours, to do so chiefly by their power of seeing the truth and by their courage and ability in telling it. He was himself so unmistakably a man of genius that the fact for that reason had escaped his notice. No incense was ever offered in the temples of his leisure. He was at ease with every hearty enjoyer of life, and any man who could do anything, and had a pipe about him, might walk up to him and talk. He had a strong and unaffected liking, which was returned, for the average man; and was frequently heard to declare that the best club in the world, and the best academy of manners, was a third-class carriage. Only in literature he was incurably aristocratic. The average man was all very well, but the average book, 'the book which does not pretend to be any better than its neighbours,' who would be left alone with? His own writing was occasional, and as a rule he would always rather talk than write. In writing, the dialogue which he loved must be conducted in silence within a single mind; and there was, besides, the imprisonment of print. Writing seemed to him like talking upon oath, and he chose for the performance of it 'courageous moments.' When he wrote it was chiefly to unload his mind or to please his friends; and the task was performed at speed and in a mood of high excitement. He believed that no enduring literary work can be otherwise produced.

It must be counted as supremely happy accident in the academic history of this country that such a man should have been captured, in the first vagrancy of his powers, and committed to the teaching trade. His good fortune is less certain, and yet he liked it, and was jovially happy and successful. Literature no doubt lost something; he once said that he should have been thrown young into a garret, to sink or swim. Alma Mater was so very motherly, and had, besides, such very odd relations! The experiment, as he must have regarded it, was a success from the first; as time went on his triumph became regal. He was a Prince of Professors, imparting to a profession not notoriously adventurous something of the gallantry and adventure of the arts. His methods, in this as in other things, were his own. He put little trust in the mechanical devices of education; and rigorous minds, to whom the roundness of the world is bewildering, found him, on occasion, a little difficult to grasp. He could seldom refuse himself 'that sudden appeal to universal considerations which is called philosophy or humour.' He had a disconcerting way, at meetings of the academical poultry show, of reminding the judges that the claims of the nightingale had been unaccountably overlooked. It was observed at the same time, that his dreams had an astonishing habit of coming true. The Oxford School of English, as it now stands, was conceived by him, and in the magnanimity of its outlines, though there have been many builders, is almost his personal creation. The impossibility of 'teaching' literature, or of elucidating it fully to auditors who have just begun to live, was alternately his amusement and despair. 'You might as well try to teach people to fall in love.' Given truth and simplicity, indeed, one might do something; and in short, 'if any young man could find a society where people speak only what they think and tell only what they know—in the first words that come to hand—that would be, at last, a School of Literature.' In his youth he had been much and brilliantly concerned with the question: 'Should a thing be said that way or this?' As he grew older, he was more often inclined to ask the previous question: 'Why should the thing be said at all? Why write anything?' It is an awkward question in any literary community; and universities, he would sometimes complain, accept and encourage very inadequate answers to it.

His friends, the compilers of these answers, had they heard him, would not have complained. He was adored by the young. The undergraduate vision of the towering lectern and the galleon's sail only faintly heightens their waking image of him. Until the war took possession of his mind, he had the quality of all others the most engaging to youth: he appeared never to be preoccupied. In a society which is perpetually consulting its diary he alone seemed free, and to anything that friendship or adventure might suggest presented always an expectant and youthful alacrity. He was, in his time, by far the most brilliant ambassador of his generation to the heart of the next. To meet a pupil of Raleigh's any time these thirty years, and only name him, was to bring a gleam into the dullest face. He will be missed in the High, and in all the happy Oxford meeting-places, but principally for that greeting when he had eyed a friend far off and his arm shot up like a mast. The houses and the little people seemed to fall away, as he bore down. It was like the speaking of a ship at sea.

It is characteristic of this lover of reality that much of his best criticism and most passionate thinking was the product of his latest years. It is equally characteristic of a public to which he never made advances that little of this work is known. His *Six Essays on Johnson* of twelve years ago comes near to being his best book. It discovered Johnson to Johnsonians, and demonstrated to a stubborn but weakening public that *The Rambler* is 'one of the most moving of books.' In his *England and the War* he will be found, when the book is read, to have come very near to discovering England. The study of England and the English character was his favourite pursuit for many years before the war, and the war, to him, was the revelation of England: his Englishman come true. These papers are written in a style which did not come by chance, or by literary purgations. It is plain and noble, and moves, like the style of Dryden, with the ease of an athlete. It is his talk at last, run free. He had come to believe more strongly that there is no finer literary model than bare matter of fact, and to rest more securely on 'that temperate show of objects that endure.' Of these objects he was proud to think that the English character is one. He was in all his work singularly modest about himself, and believed the desire for posthumous fame to be an uncommon frailty. 'Some authors seem to expect fame,' he said; 'I shall be satisfied with forgiveness.' It is nevertheless true that of all who for the last hundred years have practised the art of criticism, or, as he would himself have put it, have 'aspired to the second prizes,' there is none to be compared with him for understanding of the very voice and soul of England, none for whom Lamb and Hazlitt would so readily make room at the Thursday nights of Elysium.

THE CANT OF THE CRITIC

WHEN I think about critics I find nothing so soothing as that justly famous 55th chapter of *Tristram Shandy* which contains the celebrated curse of Bishop Ernulfus: the most thorough, searching, absolute and impartial curse in literature. It was among the favourite reading of the elder Shandy, and it shocked Captain Toby: '"I declare," quoth my uncle Toby, "my heart could not let me curse the devil himself with so much bitterness."'

Can it be by accident that Tristram slips straight from the curse in his 55th chapter into the subject of critics in his 56th? There is a justice in this too refined to be the work of chance. 'Grant me patience, just heaven!' cries Tristram, in an agony: 'Grant me patience, just heaven!—Of all the cants which are canted in this canting world—though the cant of hypocrites may be the worst—the cant of criticism is the most tormenting! I would go fifty miles on foot, for I have not a horse worth riding on, to kiss the hand of that man whose generous heart will give up the reins of his imagination into his author's hands—be pleased he knows not why, and cares not wherefore.'

There are three worlds in literature, three circles, and though they intersect, they remain three. They are the world of writers, the world of interpreters, and the world of readers.

Every liberal trade or profession has a cant proper and peculiar to itself: a familiar and often technical language in which the practitioners of the trade express themselves to each other when they are by themselves. This is not the Cant that angered Sterne and that angers me. This is as right and proper as the 'little language' of children, and it is right and proper for the same reason, because it is the language of serious people engaged in doing and making things, with which the whole of the rest of the world has no practical concern until they are done or made. In this first world, the world of artists, whether in words or colour or stone, the first and consuming concern is to make something; and, of course, while they are making things, they talk to each other about it, and of course this is criticism, the best there is. The intimate talk of artists, poets, doctors, and all craftsmen is of this sort; and the public has properly nothing to do with it. Indeed I doubt if it is good for the general public to hear such talk at all. Sometimes it slips through and comes to the public ear, on which it makes, as a rule, a very disappointing impression. For it has a curious character.

It will nearly always be found to be practical and unemotional, and this cannot fail to disappoint a public which brings to these matters a great fund, no doubt, of general intelligence, but primarily and above all a hungering and warm heart. But the very basis of all such intimate talk is that the warm heart, sentiment, sympathy and the rest shall be assumed, and never, except on the rarest occasions, so much as mentioned. What could be harder or more unfeeling, nor, in itself, more wholly satisfactory, than the talk of two painters about a sunset or of two doctors about a disease? Not so much as a flush or a sigh between them! A feeling for the beauty of Nature, a sympathy for pain, is assumed among them. It was this, presumably, that took them out of the public to be painters and doctors; their concern thereafter is to be proficient in their art. The young doctor is still an ordinary member of the public when he faints at his first visit to the operating theatre. That over, he is an ordinary member of the public no longer, but a member of a fraternity and the practitioner of a craft. To expect the painter or the poet to be normally burning with the hidden passions of his calling and willing to proclaim them, is as absurd as to expect the doctor to be on the point of fainting sympathy at every operation. The public sees the folly of the last expectation, because the art of the doctor affects its person; it does not, and perhaps never will, see the folly of the first and equally unnatural expectation, because the art of the painter and the poet touches it in none of those parts which it thinks vital, but is regarded as a kind of ingenuity to be encouraged for the honour of its soul. There is a sentence in one of Edward FitzGerald's letters which gives you the whole thing at once. Tennyson had just published his *In Memoriam*, and Fitz-Gerald, his friend and fellow-artist, mentions the publication to a common friend. 'I hear,' he says, 'that Alfred has just published his Elegiacs on A. Hallam.' This is the language of one man of letters about another. There is no fervour about it: nothing that the critic supplies and the public likes.

All great men, I suppose, have suffered from their inter-viewers. I have a striking example from an American journal. It is the record of an interview, and though it does not concern literature, it is in the same kingdom; it is concerned with invention and the arts. A typical reporter of the American type—a believer in culture and world-souls—calls upon Edison the inventor. He has read about great men, but he has never met one, and he does not know the first principle of greatness, that it is practical and plain. Instead of asking Edison about himself, he asks him about his soul.

Q. What frame of mind helps to bring ideas?
A. Ambitious.

Q. Is it true that an inventor has to be more or less abnormal?
A. Abnormal people are never commercial inventors.

Q. Do you consider the end for which an instrument is designed, or the immediate effect you wish to produce?
A. Consider always if the public wants the invention—its commercial value.

Q. What is the chief inspiration of an inventor?
A. If he is a good inventor, it is to make his invention earn money to permit him to indulge in more inventions. If he is a one-idea inventor, the incentive is generally money only. . . . (Then to finish off the topic) Do you want to know my definition for successful invention? It is something so practical that a Polish Jew will buy it. 'This,' the interviewer remarks, 'I found was to be a keynote to his whole attitude—a con-sideration of the practical. He said that he "just works

along." It was not exactly the kind of psychological secret I had expected to find, to account for his deep insight into things. But I was interested to know what kind of ideas he would have about big things—the laws of the universe and our relations to them.'

So question and answer began again:

Q. Is a settled conception of the universe important as a background for deep thinking? ('I had heard it said,' the reporter confides, 'that a man needs to have his mind fairly at rest on the big points of life before he can do much creative work.') Edison waived the question [says the interviewer], and smiled as he said:

A. No: I always keep within a few feet of the earth's surface all the time. At least I never let my thoughts run up higher than the Himalayas. All my work is rather earthy.

Need I press home the lesson? It is an allegory of all the minor criticism of all the arts.

I have described the first of my three worlds and the tone of its talk—the good Cant which is part of the rules of a game, laid down by the experts and artists themselves. It is all simple, plain and severe. The first sign of corruption appears when the public is allowed a voice in altering the rules. It comes about by an act of bribery when the artist is tempted to leave his study or his studio and the society of his fraternity, and come on to the platform of the public. It begins, that is to say, with public criticism: which is, in the first instance, an attempt to explain the processes of creation to non-creative minds. So long as he sticks to his work and theorizes within his fraternity the artist is in no danger. The danger comes when, in order to be intelligible and attractive to the general public, he adopts its language. To be understood he is compelled to a reverse order. What he assumed in silence among his companions and fellow-practitioners, he is now compelled to put in the forefront of his discourse. Then that happens which, when it has once happened, cannot be stopped. The public appetite, once roused, continues to demand satisfaction; and since the artist cannot be on the platform for long if he is to remain an artist, a secondary race of men steps in to supply his place. These are the indefatigable friends or appreciators of genius, the men of a little talent, sympathetic men: in short, the Professional Critics.

It is a pitiful thing to see the average critic getting to work on a great man. I am not thinking now of the hodmen of literature, who flood the world with dissertations. They have at any rate a certain humility. They know instinctively that the front door of literature is not for them. They go round by the back and count the message-boys; and we pet them, and make much of them, and say that never before have the sources of such and such an author been so thoroughly investigated. I have no quarrel with these men if they keep their place. It is the front-door critic who is oppressive, the critic who assumes the man of letters, and affects to interpret great men to us. Out of many signs by which you may know him I will name only two:

Everything to this kind of critic is like (or unlike) something else. Keats writes a line—'How Shakespearian!' 'Here Keats strikes a Shakespearian note.' He writes another line—this time it is 'How Miltonic!' 'Here Keats strikes a Miltonic note.' It is the same with authors. No author is himself, he is always like someone else. The greater the poet the more people and things he must be like. 'I have seen myself compared,' said Byron,[1] 'personally or poetically, in English, French, German (as interpreted to me), Italian and Portuguese, within these nine years to Rousseau, Goethe, Young, Aretine, Timon of Athens, Dante, Petrarch, "an alabaster vase lighted up within," Satan, Shakespeare, Buonaparte, Tiberius, Aeschylus, Sophocles, Euripides, Harlequin, the Clown, Sternhold and Hopkins, to the phantasmagoria, to Henry the Eighth, to Chenier, to Mirabeau, to young R. Dallas (the schoolboy), to Michael Angelo, to Raphael, to a *petit maître*, to Diogenes, to Childe Harold, to Lara, and the Count in Beppo, to Milton, to Pope, to Dryden, to Burns, to Savage, to Chatterton, to "oft have I heard of thee, my Lord Biron" in Shakespeare, to Churchill the poet, to Kean

---

[1] From one of Byron's Journals (Moore's *Byron*, p. 644).

the actor, to Alfieri, etc., etc., etc.' Byron went on to add: 'The object of so many contradictory comparisons must probably be like something different from them all; but what *that* is, is more than *I* know, or anybody else.'

It will be found that what critics of this sort write of one man may equally well be applied to another. Indeed, I recommend it as a good test: to see how far what is written applies to the author interpreted and to no other. Many pages of the more romantic writers of last century, and even of this, can be transferred from author to author; it is a very common sign of a bad critic.

The other great mistake the average critic makes—and you may know him by it—is to write as if an author were perpetually in that frame of mind in which he wrote his works. Being of another grade of mind themselves, they cannot understand how literature—and especially poetry—is produced: that the best things in literature are the expression of rare and excited periods in a life otherwise employed. Their heroes must be always heroic. We shall never know the full extent of the mortification which the critics felt because Browning, even when he was writing the most abstruse of his works, *would* look and talk like a banker. It pained them; it pains them still. The fact is that almost all the tragic and gloomy writers have been mirthful persons in society, and almost all the humorous writers inclined to melancholy. The author of the *Night Thoughts* was, we are told, a fellow of infinite jest, and of the pathetic Rowe, whose tragedies made all London weep, Pope says: 'He! why, he would laugh all day long—he would do nothing else but laugh.' When Byron was living at Ravenna he was visited by a young admirer from Boston: 'I was very civil to him during his few hours' stay, and talked with him much of Irving, whose writings are my delight. But I suspect that he did not take quite so much to me, from his having expected to meet a misanthropical gentleman, in wolf-skin breeches, and answering in fierce monosyllables, instead of a man of this world. I can never get people to understand that poetry is the expression of *excited passion*, and that there is no such thing as a life of

172

passion, any more than a continuous earthquake, or an eternal fever. Besides, who would ever *shave* themselves in such a state?' Life must go on.

For a long time the author was his own critic, as he should always be. He wrote a preface telling the public what it had to expect and what his aim was in writing the book. It is wonderful how well it served. Though it is true that books in former times were publicly valued or decried on moral or didactic grounds, it is quite untrue that writers wrote their books without freedom and with an eye always on the moral book-buyer. No. The author, being his own critic, very quietly tricked the public. He wrote his book, and then, when it was ready for the printer, whatever the subject of his book or the manner of his writing—he very demurely strung together a number of texts from the Bible and the Fathers, and prayed for the health of his readers' souls. This was all that was wanted. The public then sat down contentedly to read whatever was written by so godly and well-wishing an author. There is nothing the public cannot stand if you only make the sign of the cross over it first. This is how Caxton and Berners, in the fifteenth century, at the very beginning of printed books in England, and Sidney and Spenser in the sixteenth, recommended their Romances of Chivalry to a puritanically-minded public. Sidney defends the romancing of the past by reminding the public that poets were the first priests and lawgivers: an *argumentum ad hominem* with a vengeance. Spenser recommends the *Faerie Queene* to the public by calling it a moral allegory, and a scheme of the twelve virtues—how to make a gentleman. Caxton and Berners, who lived in a harder age, had to hammer more loudly. They have one topic in common. They both pretend that they undertook their work out of a moral resolve—the resolve to obey the commandment of Solomon, and eschew idleness. 'When I remember,' says Caxton, in the preface to his book of the Famous Histories of Troy, 'that every man is bounden by the commandment and counsel of the wise man to eschew sloth and idleness, which is mother and nourisher of vices, and ought to put myself unto virtuous occupation and business, then I, having no great charge of occupation (he was then Governor of the English merchants in the Low Countries! a most onerous post), following the said counsel, took a French book, and read therein many strange and marvellous histories, wherein I had great pleasure and delight.' You see, the true reason slips out: he loved a story.

The same refrain comes over and over again in his prefaces and epilogues, like a catchphrase mumbled by rote: 'in eschewing of idleness, mother of all vices.' In one of them,[1] when he had just been talking with ill-concealed gusto of the destruction of 'that noble city of Troy, and the death of so many noble princes, as Kings, Dukes, Earls, barons, knights, and common people'—you can see how he loves the list—he breaks off quite suddenly into a moral, as if he had caught himself only in time: 'which may be example to all men during the world how dreadful and jeopardous it is to begin a war, and what harms, losses, and death followeth. Therefore,' he goes on (with the wonderful irrelevance of thoughtless piety): 'Therefore, the Apostle saith: "All that is written is written to our doctrine," which doctrine for the common weal I beseech God may be taken in such place and time as shall be most needful in increasing of peace, love, and charity; which grant us He that suffered for the same to be crucified on the rood tree. And say we all Amen for charity!' This is how the minstrels used to end their tales of easy love and hard fighting: it soothed the conscience of their audience like a dismissing prayer.

Berners' prefaces to his *Froissart* and his *Huon of Bordeaux* are in precisely the same strain and even the same phrases; only he has the candour to put the 'delectableness' of the stories first.

I do not deny that Caxton and Berners may have felt something of this moral strain, like their public: but it was only for the moment, and for a purpose. They tricked the public for its good and their own. To-day, I am afraid, this is much more difficult; not because the public is so much more

---

[1] The Epilogue to the Third Book of his translations of the *Recuyell of the Historyes of Troye*.

enlightened (it is only larger), but because the Critics are no longer the Authors themselves, but a body of tribunes who intercept everything: who speak for the people, and flatter them by transforming their prejudices into criterion of good writing.

In the seventeenth century this tricking of a too solemn public went on merrily. The public is always inclined to make the mistake of supposing that serious work can be done only on serious subjects: a huge and intolerable mistake. Desiring to write Romances of Love, authors soothed the public, and the magistrates and knights of the city, into compliance, by representing love in their prefaces as the most serious philosophy of life and the only frame on which to form a gentleman. In this way, at the expense of a few words, the authors had their say. No critics were wanted. Authors and readers came together much better without them.

The first great English writer who took the public into his confidence about the principles of good writing was Dryden, and he lived to repent it. 'I have taught the age too well,' he said, 'how to criticize their betters.' The Dick Minims of the coffee-houses were set up for life on the catchwords of the great man.

It is common to call Dryden the 'Father of English Criticism.' If you look round the critics of the nineteenth century you will find some difficulty, I imagine, in tracing the features of the Father in his offspring. For you must note that Dryden, and indeed all his contemporaries who wrote criticisms, were critics only by accident. They were critics only as they happened to be authors. Their critiques were prefaces to their own works; written, partly to clear their own minds, partly to account to themselves and the public for their literary methods. Their criticisms, in short, were personal pamphlets, not receptive and appreciative studies.

You will see this best if you will look at their remarks about their predecessors: let us say, about Shakespeare. They often talk about Shakespeare: and it is taken as a great grievance by the nineteenth century critics, and as a great proof of the enormous advance we have made upon Dryden's time, that when they do talk of Shakespeare, they talk of him so coolly. They even catalogue his faults: and indeed sometimes they seem to dwell more upon his faults than upon his merits. And altogether there is a lack of sublimity about their admiration, and of fervour in their adulation, that seems to argue a certain blindness to the man whom Coleridge so characteristically called 'the divine one, the morning star of poetry and of philosophy.'

But what Coleridge and his successors failed to see was this: that all these writers were working dramatists, and that their criticism was incidental to their work as playwrights. When they read Shakespeare, Jonson, and Fletcher, what they looked for was the secret of their power. They were their pupils: we are only their students. They wished to learn how to do it themselves: all we wish to learn is how to admire them discreetly to the best advantage. We read them to be better men: they also read them, no doubt, to be better men (they took that for granted, and said little about it), but chiefly to be better dramatists and better poets. It was still possible to think of Shakespeare as a rival: always, at any rate, as a fellow-author. Dryden felt a secret shame when he compared his work with Shakespeare's: and so late as 1765 it was still possible for Goldsmith to confess that he envied him.

Now this, I maintain, is healthy, and the true way to criticism. It is possible to feel too far below your subject as well as too far above it. What is wrong with the criticism of the nineteenth century since the Great Romantics, and especially since Coleridge, is that in the presence of the great names of our literature our critics walk without freedom, confidence, or equality, like members of the public, and not like members of the great fraternity of authors. Until authors recover again their uncorrupted state, shake off the gaping public, and its tribunes and mouthpieces, the student-critics, we shall never rival either the grandeurs of our past literature or the just dignity and reticence of our older critics.

SOME POST-WAR REFLECTIONS
ON LITERATURE

IT is strange to recall, at this time of day, the extraordinary scramble of various interests and activities in England, after the First World War, for public attention and public money: literary, artistic, religious, scientific and educational interests all clamouring and competing with one another for an increased share of national esteem and of the conjectured contents of the public purse. It was an unseemly scramble, on which none of the interests involved can now look back, I should suppose, with any pleasure. The War was hardly over —many of the soldiers had not yet returned—when it became apparent that it had been won by everybody. The Chemists and Physicists had won it; ergo let laboratories be unlimited, and down with Greek! The Public-Schoolboy had won it, straight from his cricket and his construing; so hurrah for the playing-fields, and why change anything? The Working Man had won it; and this was nearer the truth than most of these contentions; but the conclusion, Down with Capital! seemed hastily drawn. It was won, also, by the Church, and chaplains were forthcoming, familiar with the rest-camps of Étaples and Rouen, who testified to the extraordinary piety of the British private soldier, as evidenced by his readiness to sing hymns in mid-winter in warm huts which provided hot coffee. A religious revival was accordingly predicted, and we were asked to subscribe the means for sustaining it. There were also our War Poets, some of whom, but not all, were good soldiers. Could not Poetry, and Literature generally, make something out of that? For several years, until the new voices came, and the old tunes went flat, Poetry did very well out of it, and, under a banner commandingly inscribed with the romantic name of Rupert Brooke, sheltered a considerable number of young or youngish poets who had never known a foreign field, and were better acquainted with the book-market than with either soldiering or civics. There were also, in the educational world, answering the scientists, and in-deed the modernists of whatever shade, the ancient claims of the Classics, and anecdotes were told of young officers who could produce, if required, weather-beaten copies of Homers or Horaces which they had carried everywhere about with them, and had even read in what were loosely called 'the trenches.' But they in turn were outfaced by the naturally far greater number who had carried into action an India-paper Shakespeare, or Shelley, or Keats. It used, in the old days, to be a copy of the Bible in which a bullet had miraculously embedded itself; but our pocket-companions had grown secular, like the age. I should be the last to throw discredit on these literary devotions, though I was never happy enough to share them. I am one of, I fancy, a considerable number of ex-infantry officers who found, on the contrary, how easy it was, in such scenes and in such company, to live without reading at all. Literature fell into place. The bookworm, indeed, was almost the only kind of creeping thing that I have no recollection of ever meeting on service.

I have sometimes wondered, none the less, how persons bred to reading and the life of books, should for four years on end have done so well without them. The chief reason, I suppose, is that books, in most of their forms, are a kind of shorthand for multiplying experience. If your own experiences are new and full enough, you hardly need books. Literature is so powerful and splendid a thing, it is or can be so en-trancing, and reading is so much a habit, that we are in danger of forgetting our natural independence of it. Have we not five senses, and is not the world before us? Only two can be employed in reading, and for the most part, nowadays, we employ only one. I should like to advocate occasional periods of fasting from all literature, and a more resolute and direct reliance, for imaginative experience, on ourselves. The mirror of our minds would be clearer, if, for a month now and then, no writer breathed upon it, and we should be fitter, when we returned, to compare his finished and printed experience with the raw material of our own. We should really have some experience which we knew to be our own, and our reading would take a livelier character.

No book was ever the same to two readers, or remains the same to any reader for any length of time. Books change, like places, because we see them differently, and many of them changed very abruptly with the War. There was a shifting of values, among books as among men, from which some are only now recovering, and from which some, perhaps, will not recover in our time. The weaker sort of romantics, who were very near the grave when the War broke out, the long-haired men, dropped plump out of sight as useless, and all the little loungers and conceited triflers of literature, the foolish egotists and poor leavings of Art-for-Arts'-sake, dropped unregretted with them. Even Stevenson, I remember, suffered as a weakling who had played at adventure. 'C.3,' I heard him called, in a brutal mood, by somebody, and thought it the shortest and harshest criticism on record. Yet I knew what was meant, and that it was not all a matter of lungs. Thackeray's vogue was in decline, no doubt, before the War, but the War finished it. Something flimsy and a little tawdry in the composition of the man, perhaps—some flaw in sentiment—was then unmercifully exposed. Such writers as Dickens, on the contrary, or Johnson, or Lamb, or the good Trollope, never budged, but, like Shakespeare, seemed to thrive and luxuriate in any circumstances. Of Shakespeare, I suppose, the War was a minor revelation; we had hardly known how true he was, or how English, before.

Of the shocks to my own reading I will mention only one. I had always been fond of Stevenson's *Travels with a Donkey*, and I remember still the pleasing rustle with which I opened it one day in 1919, after long separation, and settled myself to read. I got a very little way. I never reached, in fact, even the charming dedication to Sidney Colvin. I was transfixed by the Frontispiece. This is a picture drawn for Stevenson by Walter Crane, and depicts, in the old woodcut manner, the various stages of that somewhat befrilled but still romantic journey. It is pretty enough; but what pinned me and kept me staring was the foreground, in which Stevenson is represented, under a setting sun, in a fur-lined sleeping-bag and with a Balaclava helmet on his head, peacefully smoking, in a recumbent attitude, under a tree, and evidently preparing for a night's sleep. Nothing wrong so far. I do not even complain of the revolver lying by his side. A romantic actor must have his playthings, and must pretend there is danger even if there is none. What held me was not Stevenson, but the donkey: Modestine, tethered a few yards off to a beech-tree, and against all the laws of travel, and even of human mercy, with the heavy pack-saddle still fastened to her back, and evidently intended to remain there all night. I suppose it was a little ludicrous of me—I think so myself now, and have almost got over the incident—but when the enormity of these arrangements dawned on me I put the book down, and turned with impatience from the reminiscences of a traveller who did not know the decent elements of his business. That Crane drew it and not Stevenson was no defence, for Stevenson passed it; and indeed it seems confirmed by the narrative. I tell this story at length, because it illustrates an unexpected effect of army service. I must have looked at that picture fifty times before without seeing anything wrong, and never should have seen it if I had not learned in the interval how pack animals should be treated on the march.

But I am constantly finding that some experience of the War enlightens, or shows up, my reading. Even for a peaceful man of letters, as Gibbon found, it is worth while to have been for a time a soldier.

The effect of the War on the reputation of dead writers is easier to speak of than its effect on the living. On most of our representative English writers past forty years of age the War came with stunning force. Many of them, at first, could hardly be brought to understand, especially the more successful of them. If one wrote something, they seemed to think, in one's very best style, and got all the other writers with large audiences to sign it, surely something could still be done! There was actually a literary album produced, full of gush and rant, and signed by these people in December 1914, for presentation to the King of the Belgians. It was apropos of this performance, which he had been asked to sign, that the late Walter Raleigh wrote one of his best and shortest letters. 'Dear Sir,' he replied, 'The best present to give to the King of the Belgians is Belgium. Two of the men of this household are at the front, and the third is drilling. Yours truly.' Words, it soon became clear, had gone down in price, and presently the authors fell silent. A gloom descended on the fraternity; they felt that they didn't matter, and some of them could hardly bear it. The good ones got over it and did their duty, whatever it was; the conceited sulked; but some have never quite recovered from the awful suspicion of that time, the suspicion that literature was futile. The same agony of doubt was suffered by French authors, and with far more reason, after the Franco-Prussian War. A whole race of writers was broken then—Michelet, Flaubert and the rest. They ceased to believe in what they were doing: 'Flute-players,' cried one of them, 'drowned by the trumpets!'— and threw down his pen. Since England became a nation we have never endured so bitter an experience as that; but even as it was, the confidence of authorship was torn. With most of our writers already established and set in their ways the War dealt hardly.

I was looking the other day at the well-known cartoon of Max Beerbohm's, which depicts the English literary world before the War. Robert Louis Stevenson is represented in it as returning from the Shades, and as accompanied on his tour by certainly the best of all possible *couriers*, Mr. (as he then was) Edmund Gosse. Stevenson, lean, long-haired, and velvet-jacketed, regards with a faint romantic interest a group of figures which fill the rest of the picture, in all the various attitudes and gesticulations of the platform. We recognize them at once; the short stumpy figure of Mr. Wells, looking as if he had stolen another man's head; the easy provocative figure of Mr. Bernard Shaw, cocking his red beard (it was still red) at the world; the Gallic form of Mr. Belloc, exuding eloquence and force, an English Mirabeau; the melancholy-eyed exile, Mr. Yeats; and behind them all, towering like a figure of Velasquez, the massive shape of Mr. Chesterton, in an ulster and pince-nez—all waving their hands, and gesticulating, and propagandizing to their hearts' content. Mr. Wells has a tub to stand on, out of deference to his size; but Mr. Chesterton is his own tumbril. 'Very interesting,' says Stevenson, 'very interesting indeed; but show me your men of letters.' 'These *are* our men of letters,' said Mr. Gosse.

They still are, I am glad to say, all of them; but you can understand what it meant to some of them when the War blew up their platforms, and stole their audiences. For they had all turned publicist together. They are none of them now quite the men they were, and not merely because they are older, but because something happened to them, and because the world is different. Their stride was broken, and the racecourse now has other obstacles and younger hurdlers.

I think, on the whole, that the books now being written in England on any subject with which I am acquainted are better written, and better books, than in the corresponding period before the War. Some of our scientists, philosophers and historians are writing now with the skill and elegance of men of letters, and men of letters have widened their outlook, and are reading and taking account of what science and philosophy have got to say. Literature is expanding again and taking in its lost domains. Half the novelists and poets of England—of the writers who matter—are curious about scholarship, or deep in psychology and anthropology. It is a remarkable change and can do nothing but good. There was a time before the War when Literature was at feud with all the specialists, and when all the specialists suspected Literature. Our novelists and essayists and men of letters generally affected to despise learning, spoke loudly of Mandarins and Mr. Dryasdust, and used 'scholarly' and 'scientific' almost as terms of abuse. The scholars and scientists not unnaturally retorted, and any one of their number who wrote a better style than usual ran the risk of being insulted by having his work described as 'literary.' It was a lamentable division in the republic of letters, and I look upon the signs that it is on the way to being healed as among the most encouraging of the present time.

There are to be found, of course, in the work of great scientists stylistic powers and elegances which owe nothing to literature. I quote Ludwig Boltzmann, a scientist of Vienna:[1]

'As the musician, from the first bars, recognizes Mozart, Beethoven or Schubert, so would the mathematician distinguish, after only a few pages, his Cauchy, Gauss, Jacobi and Helmholtz. Great outward elegance, together with a certain weakness of structure, marks the French, supreme dramatic power the English, Maxwell in particular. Who does not know his Dynamical Theory of Gases? First of all the variations of the velocities unfold themselves with majesty; then from one side fall in the equations of state, from the other the equations of central motion; higher and higher surges the chaos of formulae; suddenly the four words ring out: "Put $n=5$." The evil demon V vanishes, as in music a wild disturbing bassfigure suddenly falls silent; as by a stroke of magic that which before seemed insuperable falls into order. Then is not the time to ask why this or that substitution is made: let him who does not feel it lay the book aside; Maxwell is no programme musician bound to explain his notes.'

One does not need to be a scientist to recognize here that same excitement of the mind as one is familiar with in the presence of all great art. Here, once again, are affinities which our age might explore.

I began by speaking of the scramble of claims that assailed the English nation after the War. Most of the contestants, even education which was the shrillest of all, have now fortunately subsided and settled down to their proper business and to their natural proportions in the life of the community. Even Poetry for some time has ceased pretending to be Religious, or, if not Religious, the only modern substitute for it. Religion in England is much occupied to-day with discipline, and that, of course, is the usurper's chance. But Poetry has not come forward, as from time to time she does, with offers to deputize, or with competing and seductive praises of

[1] *Populäre Schriften*: Leipzig, 1905.

her mysterious divinity. The reason, or one reason, is that Poetry in England is occupied with discipline also, and has as many points of doctrine to settle as the Church. In both, for the moment, Vision is in abeyance, and the concern is with Technique. Our poets are inspecting not only the technique, but the validity of their art. What is this inspiration which poets have claimed, and with what authority does it come? How, they ask Psychology, are poets created, and with what ground of truth? Once more I see a *rapprochement* with science. 'Science and poetry,' says one of the oracles of the new school, 'have but one ideal.' 'Facts,' says another, 'cannot hurt taste.' As for technique, we are telling ourselves in England that we must be patient with our new poets. If the accustomed magic is absent from their poetry, presumably they are searching for some other. They are an orchestra, tuning up, and that, as you know, means odd noises. The great point is that they are working, and not waiting for some Deity to do their work for them.

ROBERT BRIDGES

THE death nine months ago of Robert Bridges, however deeply we may grudge it, coming when it did, in his 86th year, in the full glow of a last magnificent accomplishment, must be counted happy. His friends had observed, as the *Testament of Beauty* neared completion, a growing anxiety to reach the end, and make up his account at once with art and nature. Habitual as its speculations had become to him, and easily as it moves in its 'loose Alexandrines,' now like a hale old countryman in clouted shoon, now like some pacing patriarch, so sustained a performance must have tried a younger man, and it seems that he feared some sudden failure of strength. As it proved, he not only finished the *Testament*, but lived to revise it, and to enjoy unaffectedly, as indeed he enjoyed everything, the glow of a public approbation so warm and home-felt that even his memory could not have supplied a modern parallel. The barrier of reserve between a nation accustomed to more accommodating officials and a Laureate who was first of all a private gentleman broke down before the conjunction of this unexpected masterpiece and an 85th birthday. One of his chief satisfactions was in the sale of the poem, for he had always wished, and now more than ever, to be read.

It was difficult to believe, on meeting Mr. Bridges, so easily did he breathe our biting modern air, that he was born in the first decade of the reign of Queen Victoria, and learned his letters in the Laureateship of Wordsworth. He was so frankly and vitally there before you, with such challenge in voice and eye, and in the whole splendid length of him, shaggy-crowned, such lounging and half-arrogant power. Even that atmosphere which lay about him as of some ampler, more leisured, and now vanished age, hardly prepared one for the discovery that he had been familiar as a child with the sight of the Great Duke (a valued memory), and had watched, as a boy of ten, from a Walmer garden, the departure of Napier's fleet for the Baltic under the new power of steam— in those days when first was seen

> low and black
> Beside the full-rigg'd mast the strange smoke-stack.

There must have been much that he could tell about the great Victorians and their ways, but somehow one did not think to ask him. There was never a man less built for the part of mumbling ancestor. His talk was not of bygones, but of present, future, or eternal things: his work or yours, what the scientists or psychologists were doing, or the younger poets, what wireless *will* do, or if the sun shone and nature luxuriated, the life of birds and flowers, perhaps, or the principles of beauty and rightness in the conduct and the arts of man.

If it was difficult to make a Nestor of Mr. Bridges, quite another difficulty awaits the critically minded who cannot know him and have yet to read him. Posterity, it is certain, encountering his last and greatest work, will be puzzled to understand, without much more knowledge than is yet prepared for it, how a man of his generation, however favoured by longevity, should have presented to what is almost the generation of his grandchildren, not only the finest but in many ways the most representative poem of our time. This is already indeed a puzzle to numerous readers of the present day, among them old adherents, contented quoters of his lyrics, who had thought until 1930 that they knew their Bridges.

The answer to such perplexities is biography, by which I mean that history of the spiritual and artistic life which is more especially the biography of poets. It is now a fashion to study intently the youth of great poets, and there is poetical reason for it. It is in those early years that the Delphic stamp is taken. It is now well recognized that in those once *unnoticed* years of youth and childhood—for, in their biographies, our ancestors hastened always to the grown man—a poet accumulates by far the greatest and most valuable portion of the natural riches on which he is to draw for life. Bridges himself dwells on this. 'That children have an innate love of Beauty is undeniable. . . . While the intellectual faculty is still dormant, spiritual things are to children as music is, which a child readily absorbs, without thought, although a full-grown man, if he has lacked that happy initiation, can scarcely by grammar come at the elements.' In his scheme of life, indeed, as his *Testament* has revealed, he traces the hopes and prospects of mankind to the natural desire, only gradually relaxed and never wholly lost, for what is beautiful and good, which may be seen in the wondering eyes of children, and by Christian symbol, in the face of the young Christ.

The life of Robert Bridges is in neither its inner nor its outer aspects other than very imperfectly known to the present generation. This is the fate, no doubt, of men who outlive their contemporaries, and lead, besides, as Bridges did, an intensely private life. It was a fate, I may add, which he regarded with equanimity. He had hoped, or so I fancy, that he had settled with that, and closed the door on further publicity, when he fused all the thought and art and passion of his long life in the *Testament of Beauty*. There was his last confession, his sifted and essential autobiography. The effect of the poem, if I may judge by various signs, has, in fact, been just the contrary. It has brought the world at last acquainted with his life, but in such a manner that it must know more. Had he continued, as once seemed likely, to be regarded and esteemed as in the main a lyric poet, the public, no doubt, would have borne its ignorance with unconcern. But the *Testament* has changed all that; and because it is so plainly the magnificent echo of a splendid nature and the last message of a complete life, the public which has been thumbing the unexpected gospel, looks naturally for elucidation, and above all for a life of the apostle. He himself, I must think unfortunately, took another view. There was to be no official or authorized life: on that he was clear and indeed insistent. Yet somehow, by someone, from material thus necessarily imperfect, it will be done.

It is on the youth of Robert Bridges that most has been revealed to us: much may be gathered from his memoirs of others, and these and similar indications will, no doubt, some time be faithfully gathered together. In outline the biographical portrait is clear enough. He comes before us first as a boy at Eton, and happy there; to the end it is 'the beloved school'; and his Founder's Day Ode is not only the best of Eton Odes, which is saying much, but one of the best of his poems, which is saying more. He was almost *formed*, I should say, at Eton, so well it suited him, and by the time he went to Oxford had taken his mould. Fortune had been kind to him—and seldom through life relented in this benevolence—endowing him with every handsomeness of mind and body, and with the means, moreover, of future leisure. He was athlete, musician, and scholar; had the friends he wished, and had them without effort; and like many serious lads, before and since, believed himself destined for the Church. He passed to Oxford, which shared henceforth with Eton in his institutional affections; read widely and philosophically; was the best stroke of his year; and, wiser than some of his Victorian predecessors in the Laureateship, decided that even a poet should have a profession. His choice was masterly, for, being a poet, he chose science. The rest may be briefly told. After some travel in Egypt, Syria and later in Germany, he went to St. Bartholomew's Hospital and became a doctor, practised for ten years, and latterly with distinction, and only then, at thirty-eight, left the hated town for poetry and a country life. In the forty-seven years which he had still to live he remained faithful to poetry and a country life. Some twenty of his quiet middle years were spent at Yattendon, where in 1884 he married Monica, daughter of his friend Alfred Waterhouse; the rest of his days at Chilswell, the house he had built on Boar's Hill, near Oxford.

He was in practice no party to that extremity of criticism which demands that poetry shall be read without reference to its authors. There are times for that; but it will always be true, as Bridges himself has said, that 'those who admire or love a poet's work are instinctively drawn to the *man*, and are eager to learn anything that may deepen their intimacy.' In one of those fragments of autobiography which inlay his memoirs of his early friends, he has noted the precise occasion when the attractions of literature first appeared to him. 'I was eleven years of age,' he says, 'in the lower school [at Eton], in the division called Sense, when I first read Ovid, and some elegies of his opened my eyes to Poetry.' Ovid in his time has opened many eyes, but not always to art. It was his command of his medium that won this school-boy, and Bridges' natural bent for craftsmanship, for the *Art* of Poetry, became presently clear. It was brought home to him early by the different attitude of his young friend Dolben, who was a junior in the same House and, like Bridges, a furtive composer. '. . . we were mutually coy of exposing our secret productions, which were so anti-pathetically bad.' On the nature of this antipathy Mr. Bridges has an important passage. 'Our instinctive attitudes towards poetry,' he says, 'were very dissimilar, he regarded it from the emotional, and I from the artistic side; and he was thus of a much intenser poetic temperament than I, for when he began to write poetry he would never have written on any subject that did not deeply move him, nor would he attend to poetry unless it expressed his own emotions. . . . What had led me to poetry was the inexhaustible satisfaction of form, the magic of speech, lying as it seemed to me in the masterly control of the material: it was an art which I hoped to learn. An instinctive rightness was essential, but, given that, I did not suppose that the poet's emotions were in any way better than mine, nor mine than another's: and, though I should not at that time have put it in these words, I think that Dolben imagined poetic form to be the naïve outcome of peculiar personal emotion; just as one imagines in nature the universal mind conquering nature by the urgence of life—as he himself describes it in his "Core":

> Poetry, the hand that wrings
> (Bruised albeit at the strings)
> Music from the soul of things.

There is a point in art where these two ways merge and unite, but in apprenticehood they are opposite approaches.'

This is a valuable statement and is the proper preface to any account of Mr. Bridges' poetry. Dolben's assumption that emotional urgence will find or make its own form is the romantic, and also the amateur, view in all the arts, and can only be disproved by failure. Neither on this nor on one other point to which he draws attention did Bridges change. I mean his inability to suppose that the emotions of the poets he read were any better than his own, or his own than another's. Many years later, in his famous essay on Keats he reaffirms this:

'There must be thousands and thousands of persons alive at this moment in England, who, if they could only give poetic expression to those mysterious feelings with which they are moved in the presence of natural beauty, would be one and all of them greater poets than have ever yet been.' This is easily said, but Bridges meant it. What these thousands of people want, of course, is art; an art equal to that mystery. But their souls are right. No less than his respect for art is his faith in the human spirit, at whatever stage of articulation, and this was a tenet of his creed to the end. It is so declared in his last poem, and indeed is a necessity of its reasoning. I speak of it now because the thorough-paced artist, as Bridges was, has so seldom held this view. It is of a piece with his devout humanity.

The same Memoir of Dolben introduces us to Bridges at the age of seventeen, 'reading Shakespeare for the first time,' and finding, what so many schoolmasters take no account of, that his imperfect understanding 'hindered neither my enjoyment nor admiration.' He was already deep in his favourite Milton—the First Book of *Paradise Lost* had dazed him with its grandeur—and he carried Keats about with him in his pocket. The eager Dolben tried to lure him to the new poetry and fashions of the day—to Mr. and Mrs. Browning, Tennyson, Ruskin and the rest: all then in their glory, for I am speaking of 1862. But already he was exhibiting his characteristic power of refusing the wrong diet, knowing instinctively that it *was* wrong, for *him*. Ruskin: No. Tennyson: the early lyrics—he had them by heart; but not, he was sure, *The Idylls of the King*. '. . . when I heard *The Idylls of the King* praised as if they were the final attainment of all poetry, then I drew into my shell, contented to think that I might be too stupid to understand, but that I could never expect as good a pleasure from following another's taste as I got from my own.' Yet he yielded to the vogue sufficiently to choose from the *Idylls* his speech on the 4th of June, 'wherewith I indulged,' he says, 'the ears of his late majesty K. Edward VII on the year of his marriage; and I even purchased as gifts to my friends the fashionable volumes which I had never read through.' Dolben made a later attempt with *Enoch Arden*, just out in 1864. 'Are you not made happy by Tennyson's new volume? It was worth all one's long waiting and expectation indeed.' Bridges, however, had *not* been waiting, nor had he any considerable expectations from it. 'I remember reading it,' he says (in a sentence which stages him), 'without all Digby's enthusiasm, in the hot sun on a treeless cricket-field waiting for my innings.'

I dwell on these things because his life is so little known and because in essentials he changed so little, because this schoolboy of eighteen is so like the man I knew. He came to have some half a dozen languages at his command, and was a wide and intent but increasingly selective and capricious reader. There had so seldom been any reason why he should persevere with what he did not like, or open, indeed, at all, what failed to invite him. It was his one complaint against Mr. W. P. Ker that he was so catholic, that not content with the appalling self-sacrifice of reading everything, he actually tried (could it be believed?) to *like* everything also—for something. When Mr. Bridges had decided that Dryden, for example, had nothing that he wanted, it was no good speaking to him of Dryden's other abilities; he was done with Dryden. It is the difference between the reading of the scholar and the artist, even when the artist is a scholar: the mature artist, at any rate, reads not so much to enlarge his taste as to confirm or refine it. In the essay on Keats he has occasion to mention, as something generally known, the bad effect on that poet's work of the poetry of Leigh Hunt. He *makes* the statement; but a footnote assures us that he had not shared in Keats' defilement. 'I have not read Hunt's poems,' he says; why should he? What enfeebled Keats he was not called on to endure. He was to meet, in later life, various reminders of his omissions. In 1916, addressing the Tredegar Cooperative Society, he confessed, at the risk of forfeiting their confidence, as he acknowledged, that Macaulay's *Essays*—one of the best sellers of his boyhood—was still, at that date, practically a new book to him. He had found a volume of them that summer in a holiday cottage—'an inscription in it recording,' he says, 'how it had been won by its owner in a whist-drive.' He read it through, and was astonished to find Macaulay praising Shelley, and even in terms which he approved. For Browning, another urgent and elder contemporary, he had never cared, and the result is plainly seen in his famous war-time anthology. When asked why this famous poet, a sursum corda man, if ever there was one, should have been altogether omitted from *The Spirit of Man*, a volume intended to encourage, he truthfully replied, taking only the immediate question, that he supposed there wasn't a Browning in the house. This is English as well as aesthetic. I am reminded of a sentence in Professor Conington's edition of Virgil. 'The editions of the classics to which I have referred,' he says, 'have been in general the best and latest, when my library happened to contain them.' This perfectly intelligible English standpoint, that an Englishman is a private gentleman and householder *first*, and an editor or anthologist afterwards, is one that our foreign neighbours will never understand.

The result of this perfect freedom on Mr. Bridges' taste and mind has been best described by his friend Sir Walter Raleigh—Letter to Lady Elcho, October, 1912:

'Robert Bridges has just been in on the way down the hill. He is delightfully grumpy. He mentions thing after thing which is commonly believed and says that of course it's not so. He's always right. His intellect has been so completely self-indulged that it now can't understand rubbish. He has never obeyed anyone or adapted himself to anyone, so he's as clear as crystal, and can't do with fogs. He brought with him,' he goes on, 'a nice bright-eyed girl, or child, who hung on his words and thought ineffable things which played over her face like a little breeze, while we, the Old and Horny, did the talking.

What fun it would be if children had the power of speech!'

This is Bridges as he was.

It may have struck you—it struck many who knew Bridges —how little of all this masculine character, this brusqueness, this humorous self-will, is to be found in the poetry which he spent most of his life producing; the poetry by which he gradually and rightly became famous, and by which he is best known even now. What struck one about much of his earlier verse—the beautiful lyrics, odes and sonnets—was not only the perfection of their form and keeping, the exquisite insight of their observation, and the purity of their moods, but how much of himself, of the man one knew—of the man who at last spoke out in the *Testament of Beauty*—he had con- trived to keep out of them. Even his friends would remark that he was too constantly aware that the Muses are maidens. There was something in the charge. I have here the 1873 volume: of the fifty-two poems which it contained only eighteen were reprinted: and for the most part with good reason. But there are two poems which I claim to rescue here and now, the first and the last, from their author's delicacy.

> Her eye saw, her eye stumbled:
>   Her fingers spread and touched it:
> It was so ripe it tumbled
>   Off in her hand, that clutched it.
>
> She raised it up to smell it:
>   Her jealous tongue ran o'er it:
> Ere the thought rose to quell it,
>   Her keen teeth closed and tore it.

There, as she stood in wonder,
   And smacked the flavour fruity,
She scanned it o'er and under,
   And marvelled at its beauty.

'It's fair,' she said, 'and fairest
   Just where the sun's rays strike it;
The taste's the strangest, rarest;
   It's bitter, but I like it.'

To man she brought it, bitten,
   She brought it, she the woman,
The fruit, of which 'tis written
   The eating should undo man.

'Taste, taste!' she cried, 'thou starvest;
   Eat as I ate, nor fear it,
For of all the garden's harvest
   There's nothing like or near it.

'Fair to the eyes, and fairest
   Just where the sun's rays strike it:
But oh! the taste's the rarest,
   It's bitter, but thou'lt like it.'

He took the fruit she gave him,
   Took it for pain or pleasure:
There was no help could save him,
   Her measure was his measure.

Through her teeth's print, the door of it,
   He sent his own in after;
He ate rind, flesh, and core of it,
   And burst out into laughter.

''Tis fair,' he cried, 'and fairest
   Just where the sun's rays strike it:
The taste's the strangest, rarest,
   It's bitter, and I like it.'

Should it be saved? Bridges would evidently not allow this poem, either as frivolous, or too outspoken, to spoil the neighbourhood of his purer Muse.

The second is dated 1869: it also was published in the 1873 volume.

Epitaph on a Gentleman of
the Chapel Royal

Old Thunder . . . s is dead, we weep for that,
He sings for aye his lowest note, B flat.
Unpursed his mouth, empty his mighty chest,
His run is o'er, and none may bar his rest.
We hope he is not d—d, for if he be
He's on the wrong side of the middle sea.
Nay we are sure if weighed he will not fail
Against the Devil to run down the scale;
While even three-throated Cerberus must retreat
From one that bellows from his sixteen feet:
Or should he meet with Peter at the door,
He'll seize the proper key as heretofore,
And by an easy turn he'll quickly come
From common time straight to *ad libitum*.
There is the equal temperament of Heaven,
Sharps, crotchets, accidentals, all forgiven,
He'll find his place directly, and perspire
Among the bases of the Elysian quire.
   Fear, dwellers on the Earth, this acquisition
To the divine etherial ammunition;
A thunder is let loose, a very wonder
Of earthborn, pitiless, Titanic thunder:
We who remain below and hear his roar
Must kneel and tremble where we laughed before.

Bridges' answers to the charge cannot well be resisted. His first answer was that the orthodox forms, in which he excelled, did not admit of such matter. His second and final answer was the *Testament of Beauty*.

When the *Testament of Beauty* appeared in 1930 he had been publishing poetry for fifty-seven years. For a leisured man with so ripe a message it was a long time to wait. Nor is the riddle much resolved by the authentic intelligence that the *Testament of Beauty* owes nothing, as composition, to the slow garnering of years, but was an entirely fresh work, tentatively begun in 1926. Between the *Testament of Beauty* and that poetry of studied ode and delicately silvered lyric by which Mr. Bridges made his name and entered for ever the anthologies, the contrast, indeed, is striking at almost every point: as if Chaucer, abandoning the acquired metres of culture and his Legends of Good Women, should have startled Court and Custom House with 'In a somer seson' and that May-morning slumber on Malvern Hills. Consider these lines from the *Testament of Beauty*:

'Twas late in my long journey, when I had clomb to where
the path was narrowing and the company few,
a glow of childlike wonder enthral'd me, as if my sense
had come to a new birth purified, my mind enrapt
re-awakening to a fresh initiation of life;
with like surprise of joy as any man may know
who rambling wide hath turn'd, resting on some hill-top
to view the plain he has left, and see'th it now out-spredd
mapp'd at his feet, a landscape so by beauty estranged
he scarce will ken familiar haunts, nor his own home,
maybe, where far it lieth, small as a faded thought.

To the large number of readers whose only idea of Mr. Bridges was drawn from *The Growth of Love* and some of the shorter Poems, from

'My lady pleases me and I please her;
This know we both. . . .'

or

'I have loved flowers that fade'

the new style, quite apart from its accompanying swarm of thought, seemed the work of some other and more spatulous hand. But these were superficial impressions. The loose and roomy metre of the *Testament* is, in fact, the last fruit of prosodic investigation, of a series of experiments carried on by the poet with perfect frankness for many years, and to that, and that alone, we owe that the poem was ever written. This is not the usual order in the genesis of poetry, but it was Bridges' order. Had he failed to discover the metre of the *Testament*, I will not say that he would never have written his philosophy. He spoke often of doing so, sometimes, in despair, of doing it in prose. I have noticed, indeed, that his Broadcast Lecture on Poetry, given in 1929, is an advance statement of the principles of his poem. But he would not have written the *Testament of Beauty*.

That preoccupation with form which determined the natal chances of his last poem was a characteristic of Mr. Bridges all his life, and one of his principal later investigations, pursued even through the morass of quantitative hexameters, was to find a form of verse loose-limbed enough, and sufficiently capacious and accommodating to admit humour and philosophy, and generally the rambling expatiations of the mind. From 1903, when he published his poems in *Classical Prosody*, to 1921, when he wrote *Poor Poll* and its companion pieces, he was still searching for the metre in which the *Testament* is composed. It is satisfactory to see one shaft at any rate of these prosodic tunnellings, on which he was thought to waste his time, emerge in this poem into the sunlight and the approving eye of day. I believe, as he did, that his Neo-Miltonics (if only they might be called by another name!) have a great future before them in English poetry.

I cannot omit to recommend, as an adjunct to his poetry, Mr. Bridges' prose, which is admirable. Everything he wrote has in it something melodious or otherwise memorable. Though in its natural amplitude it may sometimes be thought to study nobility rather than convenience, it is a true expression of its writer, and closes always manfully with its theme. I would name more particularly his three biographies of Dolben, Canon Dixon and Henry Bradley, for he was an excellent memoirist; and also his well-known and still authoritative essay on Keats. It is the novelty of that essay that it is the criticism of a craftsman: most criticisms of such poets as Keats being only a mild and far-off raving. The usual kind of criticism would have been of no help to Keats and therefore of little interest. But he would have found technical pleasure in the method of the critic on hearing plainly that of the three short narrative poems *Isabella* is 'the worst executed'; that *The Eve of St. Agnes* 'is well done throughout,' and that *Lamia* 'is not all equally well written.' Keats and Bridges, one can see, would have understood each other. Bridges was aware of the innovation and defended himself in his concluding paragraph: 'If my criticism should seem sometimes harsh, that is, I believe, due to its being given in plain terms, a manner which I prefer, because by obliging the writer to say definitely what he means, it makes his mistakes easy to point out, and in this way the true business of criticism may be advanced.'

There is very good writing in the essay and in particular this fine passage:

'The song of the nightingale is, to the hearer, full of assertion, promise, and cheerful expectancy, and of pleading and tender passionate overflowing in long drawn-out notes, interspersed with plenty of playfulness and conscious exhibitions of musical skill. Whatever pain or sorrow may be expressed by it, it is idealized—that is, it is not the sorrow of a sufferer, but the perfect expression of sorrow by an artist, who must have felt, but is not feeling; and the ecstasy of the nightingale is stronger than its sorrow. . . .'

He had written in his own *Nightingales*:

Beautiful must be the mountains whence ye come,
And bright in the fruitful valleys the streams, wherefrom
 Ye learn your song:
Where are those starry woods? O might I wander there,
Among the flowers, which in that heavenly air
 Bloom the year long!

Nay, barren are those mountains and spent the streams:
Our song is the voice of desire, that haunts our dreams,
 A throe of the heart,
Whose pining visions dim, forbidden hopes profound,
No dying cadence nor long sigh can sound,
 For all our art.

Alone, aloud in the raptured ear of men
We pour our dark nocturnal secret; and then,
    As night is withdrawn
From these sweet-springing meads and bursting boughs of May,
Dream, while the innumerable choir of day
    Welcome the dawn.

The memoirs offer more various browsing in all modes: as this on Dolben's father: 'As he did not ride to the Pytchley, he had such a reputation as a scholar will get in a hunting district.' Or on his mother: 'Mrs. Dolben was a fine example of one of the best types of English culture: . . . such a paramount harmony of the feminine qualities as makes men think women their superiors.' Or on some early sacramental verse of Dolben's: 'The reading of these poems makes one see why schoolmasters wish their boys to play games.' On Dixon's painting: 'There exists . . . an easel-picture by him; this, hanging on the wall, might pass at a distance for one of the coloured prints published by the Arundel Society; if you go near, it reveals, indeed, a faith that should remove mountains, but also a very impressive view of the mountains which no faith can remove.' On Dixon as a curate, invariably misunderstood by his vicar and the congregation: 'We have now to think of Dixon as a curate in London: a most unusual curate. Unfortunately the idea of unlikeness to other curates gives no positive picture. . . . But if his congregation had known him better they would have understood him less.' Dixon particularly tempted him, he loved him so much: 'Like his father he was a clerical smoker indoors, and, I think, valued the use of tobacco too much to count it a luxury. His pipe lay on his writing-table in careless brotherhood with his old quill pens.'

Here I offer the reader three longer passages, as I do not know a better way of inviting him to read the memoirs:

    'Happiness cannot be measured nor even described, but its conditions at least seemed here complete.

    In one of the loveliest cities of the world—for almost all that may now hinder Oxford from holding her title is the work of the last fifty years—in a university whose antiquity and slumbering pre-eminence encourage her scholars to consider themselves the *élite* of the nation, there stood apart a company of enthusiastic spirits, in the flourish and flower of their youth, united in an ideal conspiracy to reform society by means of beauty. In the frankest friendship that man can know, when its ecstasy seems eternal, and time only an unlimited opportunity for agreeable endeavour, before experience has sobered enterprise or thought has troubled faith, these young men devoted the intention and hope of their lives to the most congenial task that they could imagine. Their light-heartedness never questioned their wisdom, and to their self-confidence all appeared as easy as the prospect was pleasant. They inherited the devotion that had built their schools and temples, and regarding the beauty that had been handed down to their enjoyment as peculiarly their own, since they alone worthily loved and adored it, they aspired to enrol themselves in the same consecration and rekindle a torpid generation with the fire that burned in their souls.'

'The summer of that year was wet in the North, and the persistent rain delaying my start made me relinquish the western end of my ramble, so it was by train that I arrived one afternoon, and first saw Dixon awaiting me on the platform of How Mill station. Emotion graved the scene on my memory; a tallish, elderly figure, its litheness lost in a slight, scholarly stoop which gave to the shoulders an appearance of heaviness, wearing unimpeachable black cloth negligently, and a low-crowned clerical hat banded with twisted silk. His attitude and gait as he walked on the platform were those of a man who, through abstraction or indifference, is but half aware of his surroundings, and his attention to the train as he gazed along the carriages to discover me had that sort of awkwardness that comes from the body not expressing the intention of the mind. His face, I saw, was dark and solemn, and as he drew near I could see that the full lips gave it a tender expression, for the beard did not hide the mouth. Nothing further could be read, only the old mystery and melancholy of the earth, and that under the heavy black brows his eyes did their angelic service to the soul without distraction. His hearty welcome was in a voice that startled me with its sonority and depth; but in its convincing sincerity there was nothing expansive or avenant. He then became so silent that I half suspected him of common tactics, and was slow to interpret his silence as mere courtesy, which it was; indeed, he would never speak unless he were assured that he was not preventing another, a habit which made a singularly untrue disguise of his eager, ingenuous temper. However, as we approached the village it was his call to talk, and he set me wondering by his anxiety that I should admire the church. It was a dreary, modern stone building with roundheaded windows and a wide slate roof; the shrunken degradation of a tower stuck on to one end and the after-concession of a brick chancel at the other. . . . I suppose he loved it as the home of his ministry.'

'Those nights I remember better than the days, of which, however, some distinct pictures remain: one is of Dixon's favourite walk in a deep combe, where the trees grew thickly and a little stream flowed by the foundations of old Roman masonry; another is a game of lawn-tennis—it could have no other name, for only the implements of that game or their approximate substitutes were used. The scene after thirty years is undimmed; I am standing with Dixon and two ladies in the bright sunlight on a small plot of grass surrounded by high laurestinus bushes in full flower, and crossed by festoons of light netting. I am more spectator than player, lazily from time to time endeavouring to place a ball where Dixon might be likely to reach it, or mischievously screwing it in order to perplex him. He like a terrier after a rat, as if there were nothing else in the world, in such rapturous earnestness that I wonder we did not play oftener.'

This last passage recalls Robert Bridges' old aristocracy of body and careless ease at games.

I must not forget Mr. Bridges' work for English speech: his lifelong and ardent interest in whatever might preserve its nobility of utterance and the significance of its sounds. He feared, not without cause, as the English language spread and wandered about the earth, a loss of grip at the centre, and it was for this reason above all that he welcomed wireless. All the crafts that concerned language were of interest to him, whether the language were to be spoken, sung, or read: he studied types and scripts like any other branch of fine art.

He felt deeply the unity of literature, of Letters. The unity of the craft of letters is an affair of the household, and operates in depth from grammarian to poet. Grammarians or critics, editors or printers, lexicographers or *vates sacri*, they were all to him 'of that ilk,' and if they vexed one another, as indeed they often do, it was a fault of temper. One of his closest and dearest friends was Dr. Henry Bradley of the Oxford English Dictionary. The Poet Laureate writing poems, and Bridges inquiring into the nature of our speech, are seen on this view to be in fact the same person working in the same material. 'The builders of the crypts,' says Mr. Ker, speaking of the Middle Ages, 'were recognized and honoured by the masters of the pinnacles; the poets in their greatest freedom of invention were loyal to the grammarians and moralists, the historians and lexicographers upon whose work they built.' Of this breed and of this polity was Bridges.

I am still left with the feeling of our loss, however due to nature, of the great Englishman he was. No man was more steadily true to himself. His physical and mental beauty matched each other, and equipped him superbly for the life he chose. He was of noble and even heroic presence, and his careless outdoor strength and grace, growing more pictur-esque with age, expressed the colour and delicacy as well as the masculine humour and outspoken freedom of his mind. He was poet, scientist, philosopher, naturalist, musician, philologist, typographer, and country gentleman—a mixture of qualities that would have been surprising in another man, and probably ineffectual, but that in him achieved their harmony. He grew up, through the kindness of fortune, un-warped by the struggle of living, with none of the inevitable vices of a profession. He used the gifts of fortune responsibly, setting an example of high-minded devotion to all the arts of Beauty and to the spiritual advancement of mankind. Before he died he delivered in the *Testament of Beauty* his message of belief in the goodness of the human heart, and of faith in the religious foundation of human life.

APPENDIX

EXTRACTS FROM NOTEBOOKS AND VARIOUS PAPERS

On The Gentility of Authorship

THE French were much quicker to become professionals than any other writers in Europe, and their authors are more professional than ours. They take their literary vocation very seriously: some of them even print 'Homme de lettres' on their visiting cards. In this country the gentleman writer kept his amateur status, and was jealous of it in work as in sport. When Congreve told Voltaire that he preferred to be considered, not as a writer, but simply as an English gentleman, he spoke for many Englishmen who were not snobs. Voltaire, the professional, did not take the point, was highly indignant, and added one more to the interminable list of our hypocrisies.

In the early decades of last century the *Edinburgh Review* still kept up the pretence that authors were really writing for fun, and these are the contortions which the editor went through when offering Christopher North a contribution fee:

My dear Sir,

I take the liberty of enclosing a draft for a very inconsiderable sum, which is the remuneration our publisher enables me to make for your valuable contribution to the last number of the *Edinburgh Review*; and though nobody can know better than I do that nothing was less in your contemplation in writing that article, it is a consequence to which you must resign yourself, as all our other regular contributors have done before you. And now, having acquitted myself of the awkward part of my office with my usual awkwardness, etc. etc.

Evidently already, since no contributor had been known to refuse, these official wrigglings were beginning to be out of date.

Biography

There was a Roman fashion of allowing the plain man to jeer at generals on their Day of Triumph. This is a type of what has happened in modern biography. We still want (I, at any rate, do) the three-decker triumphal Biography, with documents and verified references for our really interesting and great people. But the impressionistic sketch—the side-walk pointing—the jeer if necessary—have their place, as formerly in Rome. It is a mistake to suppose that they could or should supersede the more conscientious type of memorial.

True criticism is addressed to those who *know*; the newer criticism is like a cheapjack at a country fair, with this profound difference that the true critical cheapjack is often quite sincere, and believes in his own watches.

Bibliography

Our literary baggage grows terribly upon us. I have friends who cannot enter a great public library without a sense of suffocation. There are others, more executively minded, who have even dreamt of a series of carefully organized and cunningly concerted fires. But the cure is not burning, but Bibliography: and Bibliography, thank Heaven, with wonderfully increased skill and amazing perseverance, is now coming to our aid.

Literature itself has a way of relieving us. Books and authors, left to themselves, go underground, and hibernate for seasons—not all literature—not all good literature—is alive at one time. The history of literature, like the history of religion, is a history of revivals, and 'playing for revivals' is now, in some literary circles, a well-established indoor game only rivalled in popularity by that other and more questionable pastime which I may briefly and coldly refer to as 'The Limited Edition.'

No man can be a good bibliographer *in vacuo*. Bibliography is not a kind of index to be acknowledged in the preface, nor is a bibliographer some absolute thing, equally a bibliographer at all times and on all themes. This is a view of bibliography which I cannot accept. The true bibliography is something much more generous. It is not merely a sign of the historian's good faith (though it is that); it is a gift to the world of the ground he stands on. The first requisite of a bibliography on any subject is that its author shall be master of his subject.

Bibliography is not only the 'eye' of literary history—after a bookseller's catalogue, with its illicit appeal to cupidity and the gambler in man, I doubt if there be any better reading, to a prepared mind, than a good bibliography.

On Reading

The chief object of man's existence is to live, and when a man can get enough life at first hand—genuine life of mind and body, with novelty, zest, companionship and danger in it, and with all this a great and common purpose, compared to which our individual existences are nothing—books naturally fall away from him, and he becomes for the moment independent of reading altogether—so far from there being any criticism or negation of books and reading in this state of things, it has the applause of all literature. For the spirit and intention of all good reading is never reading for its own sake, but life. That life beyond reading to which all great books are for ever pointing and for which all reading may be regarded, indeed, as a preparation.

Such a life as I have described, with its temporary exaltation and independence of reading, comes seldom to any man, and when it comes, does not last. We are not constructed to live always at the pitch of crisis, and in the simultaneous exercise of all our faculties. The time comes when we tire, and fall back not ungladly, within the limits of old routine. It is at such times —which of necessity make up the greater part of our lives—that reading comes forward once more as a substitute for the larger world: a glorious Second-Best, bringing before us all that variety and richness of life, both past and present, which is beyond our reach, but not beyond our dreams.

Leeds, 1919.

On Authors and Poverty

The poverty of authors is proverbial. There have been rich authors; there are a good many now; but even of these the majority have known poverty. The typical authors of all ages are the lineal descendants of Homer, who hawked his poetry from town to town, and from castle to castle, and who collected his royalties in a hat.

One of the many troubles about the troublesome race of authors is this. They write, they will tell you, for posterity, and they expect their contemporaries to pay.

Dr. Johnson and the Provincials

'It is great impudence,' said Dr. Johnson, 'to put "Johnson's Poets" on the back of books which Johnson neither recommended nor revised.' What, then, would he have said to 'Johnson's Age'? He would not for the moment have known what to say. The locution is too modern, and the implication too tremendous for retort. Even on his own conditions it would have been difficult to reply; for, if he did not recommend the age, he could not deny that he had revised it. In an age of 'book-building' he was the master architect, and had scored more manuscripts and chastened more styles than any writer of his time. He knew everything about a book, from proposing it to binding it, and about authors, too. All the penmen of the age were familiar to him, and he to them; he had met or discussed them all; and always, in every company of authors, he was the best man in the room. In the contest of representatives (since every age must have its man) Johnson silences all claims. He was the greatest Englishman and author of his day, and so clearly and certainly these things that for the latter part of his life it was enough for him to live and be what he was. We sometimes talk as if Boswell has discovered Johnson; but there was nothing of the comet in Johnson's long and laborious career. If any man discovered Johnson it was himself, and the country took his word. It was a reputation beyond control, in which Boswell was an industrious accident; it was all settled before they met. When Boswell came to London, he came, not to support a Pretender, but to be near the throne; and his life is a Scotsman's guide to the regalia.

It is common to compare the positions of Johnson and Dryden, and the comparison is honourable to both. Dryden was the greater writer and Johnson the greater man, but they were both prime Englishmen, and by common consent the literary leaders of their time. There is, however, one great difference in their positions; the public which Dryden addressed was an English and even a London public. Johnson addressed the British Isles. His throne was London, but the provinces were his footstool, and from time to time he would make a progress through them to Oxford, or Edinburgh, or the Hebrides.

Johnson liked the Scotch, and had employed them, and had friends among them all his life. He had a value for them. But he never forgot that in any company of Scotsmen where literature is discussed the tradition is with the first Englishman who enters the room. In the new age of Britannia he stood for England and St. George, and, when he stood like that, the provincials seemed no higher than his knees. The silence of the Scotch professors when he met them in their own country was more than the silence of discretion. It was the tribute of the provincial to the greatest representative of the English race.

From *The Times Literary Supplement*, 19th December 1913.

Johnson's Lives of the Poets

The natural sequel to Boswell's *Life*, and its almost inevitable companion, is Johnson's *Lives of the Poets*. From the Boswellian album, from that incomparable picture of homely majesty and of eloquent and kindly old age, the transition is natural to the old man's greatest book—the child of his threescore years and ten, and of all his writings his own favourite and ours. Having heard him talk on men and books it seems our natural course to go on and see him write about them, for in these last years, as never before, his pen and voice went together. When we pass from Boswell to the *Lives of the Poets* we follow the same Johnson from the tavern and the drawing-room to the desk. How pleasant it is to have Johnson to ourselves: away from Boswell! These *Lives* were his last sustained performance, his final message to the world on the professional business of his life: the craft of literature, the doubtful and shifty records of the lives of authors, and the troublesome ethics—the dubious rights and wrongs—of authorship.

Printed in Great Britain
by T. and A. CONSTABLE LTD., Hopetoun Street,
Printers to the University of Edinburgh